ISRAEL
ALONE

ISRAEL
ALONE

BERNARD-HENRI LÉVY

A WICKED SON BOOK
An Imprint of Post Hill Press

Israel Alone
© 2024 by Bernard-Henri Lévy
All Rights Reserved

ISBN: 979-8-88845-783-2
ISBN (eBook): 979-8-88845-784-9

Cover design by Cody Corcoran
Interior design and composition by Greg Johnson
Translation by Steven B. Kennedy

This is a work of nonfiction. All people, locations, events, and situations are portrayed to the best of the author's memory.

Post Hill Press
New York • Nashville
wickedsonbooks.com
posthillpress.com

Published in the United States of America
3 4 5 6 7 8 9 10

Dedication

The French edition of this book, released on March 20th of this year, was dedicated to the 131 hostages still held by Hamas. Three months later, in June, with this American edition going to press, it pains me to write that the number 131 is now 120. We have had no further news of them. No one—no humanitarian organization, no "mediator" state—can tell us who among the 120 are still living and who have perished. I choose to reproduce my original dedication here, unchanged, as I keep each of these souls in my thoughts and heart.

—BERNARD-HENRI LÉVY

From the French edition:

This book is dedicated to:

Mohammad Alatrash; Liri Albag; Edan Alexander; Hisham Al-Sayed; Hamza Alziadne; Youssef Alziadne; Matan Angrest; Noa Argamani; Karina Ariev; Uriel Baruch; Ohad Ben Ami; Ron Benjamin; Agam Berger; Ziv et Gali Berman; Ariel and Kfir Bibas; Shiri and Yarden Bibas; Elkana Bohbot; Rom Braslavski; Yagev Buchshtab; Amit Ester Buskilla; Itay Chen; Eliya Cohen; Nimrod Cohen; Ariel Cunio; David Cunio; Emily Damari; Alex Dancyg; Oz Daniel; Ori Danino; Evyatar David; Sagi Dekel-Chen; Itzik Elgarat; Kaid Farhan Elkadi; Carmel Gat; Itzhak Gelerenter; Daniela Gilboa; Guy Gilboa-Dalal; Hersh Goldberg-Polin; Romi

Gonen; Maxim Herkin; Orion Hernandez-Radoux; Eitan Horn; Yair Horn; Tsachi Idan; Bipin Joshi; Ofer Kalderon; Segev Kalfon; Elad Katzir; Amiram Kooper; Andrey Kozlov; Bar Kupershtein; Naama Levy; Or Levy; Eliyakim Libman; Oded Lifshitz; Alex Lobanov; Shlomo Mansour; Almog Meir Jan; Avera Mengistsu; Yoram Metzger; Omri Miran; Eitan Abraham Mor; Gadi Moses; Avraham Munder; Omer Neutra; Tamir Nimrodi; Michel Nisenbaum; Yosef Ohana; Alon Ohel; Avinatan Or; Dror Or; Daniel Peretz; Chaim Peri; Natthaphong Pinta; Nadav Popplewell; Sonthaya Oakkharasri; Sudthisak Rinthalak; Surasak Rumnao; Lior Rodaif; Bannawat Seathao; Almog Sarusi; Eli Sharabi; Omer Shem Tov; Tal Shoham; Idan Shtivi; Keith Samuel Siegel; Watchara Sriaoun; Doron Steinbrecher; Sathian Suwankam; Pongsak Thaenna; Sasha (Alexander) Trofanov; Omer Wenkert; Yair Yaakov; Chanan Yablonka; Ohad Yahalomi; Arbel Yehoud; Dolev Yehoud; Eden Yerushalmi; Matan Zangauker; Shlomi Ziv

…who, as of February 23, 2024, remain hostages of Hamas in Gaza.

Contents

PART ONE

October 7 and After

1

Pogrom

I ARRIVED IN ISRAEL the morning after October 7.

At Ben Gurion Airport, alerts were sounding at a steady pace.

Frozen despite the late summer heat, Tel Aviv and Jerusalem seemed like dead cities.

Likewise, Sderot, a city on the Gaza border that has been martyred many times, had been emptied of nearly all of its inhabitants.

I knew this city.

I have made a point of visiting it on each of my trips to Israel over the past twenty years.

And in 2009 and 2014, during the last two Gaza wars, when people spent entire days in shelters because of the rockets, my reporting kept me there somewhat longer.

But never had I seen it so desolate.

Never had I imagined discovering, in the middle of an empty Menachem Begin Road, the remains of a dead jihadist covered with a blue tarp that left his blackened, ant-covered legs exposed and rotting in the blazing sun.

Or in front of the torched police station, of which nothing remained but the frame, finding myself face to face with my namesake, *Haaretz* journalist Gideon Levy, a virulent critic of Israel... I share my last name with many. On more than one occasion, I had the chance to get together with some others to reflect on the caprices of a "spirit of Judaism" that groups the most dissimilar Jewish destinies under the same name.

But this particular Levy.... Catching myself shaking his hand in a brotherly way and sharing an astonishment that left our disagreements behind. Gathering with him before a crowd made up of firemen, police, soldiers from the Israel Defense Forces who had arrived that morning, and reservists who showed up on their own even sooner after a parent, a friend, or a fellow reservist had called them from a safe room to confide in a whisper what may have been their last living words: "The wolves are in the city; we can sense their presence; we can hear them; they're in the yard, the living room, the children's room; as I speak, they're trying to force the lock." That, too, I never could have imagined.

In the kibbutzim, it was worse.

They had been part of my life from way back.

I knew they were the bastion of the lay, liberal, pacifist Zionism that was my first tie with Israel at the time of the Six Day War in 1967.

I had been introduced to Kfar Aza in 1967 by Ely Ben Gal, a progressive intellectual saved from the Holocaust by one of the Righteous Among the Nations in Chambon-sur-Lignon. A few days before, Ben Gal had taken Jean-Paul Sartre and Simone de Beauvoir to the kibbutz.

In neighboring Be'eri, I had stayed with Kurdish Jews whose goal was to realize their dream of reconnecting with their Arab brothers, which Saddam Hussein's tyranny had made impossible in their native Iraq.

And even though I did not arrive on the scene until after the very first reports on Israeli media, even though the teams from Zaka, the NGO whose sacred task it is to locate missing body parts so that the deceased can be given a decent Jewish burial, had come through before me and removed most of the corpses, I will never forget my first impressions: the smell of sour milk that filled the bullet-pocked, blasted, half-burned houses; the contents of their kitchen cabinets scattered in the rooms, as if blown away by a hurricane. The neatly laid out streets lined with pretty houses with their shrubs intact but empty of birdsong and human voices; or the consistent accounts of survivors and rescuers who recounted how the dead were collected, some of them decapitated and dismembered, others burned, others riddled with bullets and their hands torn to shreds as if they had fought until they dropped. Or, finally, the vegetable storage shed where unidentified body parts that had just been collected were stacked in a small pile of flesh, indistinct except for the stench.

Afterward, I met with families of the hostages. They reminded me of the parents of Gilad Shalit, whom I had visited nearly two decades before in a similar house. I pictured Ruth and Judea, the parents of Daniel Pearl, whom I met in Encino, California, in the early stages of the investigation in which I retraced the steps of the young Jewish journalist who had been abducted and beheaded. I reconstructed his last days and got as close as I could to the Al Qaeda jihadists who had murdered him so brutally. In all of these families, the same distress, the same shock, and the same difficulty in finding the right words to describe the situation. And when the words did come, the same expressions: We who survive (again, survivors) are ready to give everything, absolutely everything, even our lives, to bring back a child kidnapped without his baby bottles; a sister seen on the media, half-naked, bloodied, thrown like a package into a pickup; or a grandmother whom the abductors gave no time to say goodbye to her beloved....

And still other survivors, those of the rave and others from Be'eri evacuated to Tel Aviv, who described barbarians coming out of nowhere; the breathless, silent savagery; the stampedes; the random shootings; the motorcycles at full throttle carrying two and sometimes three attackers, the legs of the third dragging in the dust; the gray faces in which one could make out only at the last moment, in the darkness of a room, eyes gleaming with hate; the chaotic yet well-organized aspects of the whole operation, both lightning fast and very long; the babies' tears; the incredulous cries of children, eyes wide with terror; the dying, crawling toward their phone to send a last message; the phone with no charge left; a bullet in the head, one last bullet, end of story. They looked like *SS-Einsatzgruppen*, survivors told me. Never since the "holocaust by bullets" described by Father Patrick Desbois had the world seen Jews massacred like this, point blank, just for being Jewish. And, at the same time: no, I had to be careful and stifle the parade of reminiscences and images in my head. Any resemblance with an earlier situation was meaningless, because we were dealing with something utterly unique.

It is the aftermath of October 7.

My sole focus at the time was the war against Ukraine.

I had been living then on Ukrainian time for nearly two years, and the war had been consuming all of my thoughts and energy.

But at that instant, I realized with a chill that the world had just witnessed an event whose shockwaves and blast effect would change the course of all our lives—including my own.

Not all events are Events with a capital "E."

Not all have the historical, epochal, era-opening power that German philosopher Reiner Schürmann attributes to an Event.

But the pogrom of October 7, 2023 was just that—and here's why.

2

Event

AN EVENT IS DISTINGUISHED first by being unprecedented in form, says Schürmann—an underappreciated
philosopher whose work had its origins in the shadow
of the evil fairies of Nazi Germany, and particularly in
a dialogue with Martin Heidegger.

In the age of the "integrated spectacle" that Guy
Debord showed some time back to be the new organizing principle of an era that extends into the present,
the Event follows a scenario that seems to have been
written specifically for it.

As Andy Warhol epitomized by his observation that
the dream of every man, no matter how primitive, is to
be at the center of a performance that will make him
famous for fifteen minutes, the Event is more than
the latest repetition of an earlier suicide bombing, the

umpteenth hail of rockets, or the same simultaneous attack by the same allied Arab armies.

An example of an Event: Terrorists at the controls of an airplane slamming into the twin towers of the World Trade Center, symbols of power and freedom, killing 2,700 people and taking hostage hundreds of millions of Muslims who, across the centuries, had nobly embodied the adventure of their faith.

Another: Two phony journalists in Panjshir, Afghanistan, armed with a rigged camera, who blew to pieces the legendary Commander Ahmad Shah Massoud, the incarnation of enlightened Islam.

And yet another: The world's second-largest army marching toward Kyiv on February 24, 2022 and, in the process, breaking all of the written and unwritten rules of the international order since the defeat of the Nazis.

Well, the same was true of October 7, a slaughter paired with a hostage taking whose scale, savagery, and implementation resembled nothing previously known.

Israel had lived through other hostage takings: at the Olympic Stadium in Munich in September 1972; at Entebbe a short while before; and several decades later, on its own territory, when a Palestinian commando unit emerged from tunnels to capture tank commander Gilad Shalit.

Israel had experienced lynchings: those of two yeshiva students from Jerusalem who had come to worship at the tomb of Joseph in Nablus in 2015 and had to be pulled away nearly dead from a raging mob by Palestinian police; or the two IDF reservists, Josef Avrahami and Vadim Norzhich, who, in October 2000, were beaten to death, set afire, and had their remains dragged through the streets of Ramallah like Sergeant Cleveland in the last days of the battle of Mogadishu.

But both at once and at such a scale, this lynching a thousand times greater, this hostage taking without precedent since the rape of the Sabine women by Romulus's Romans, this assault by motorcycles, bulldozers, pickups, and paragliders, all by surprise and diffused in real time over social networks in posts exulting about bleeding the Jews like sheep—*that* had never happened before.

The appearance of an Event, moreover, is unpredictable.

No one sees it coming, nor even its silent stirrings.

It is the equivalent of the Black Swans whose appearance, economists say, are not foreshadowed by any datum, curve, or computation of probability or metaprobability.

"Events" are occurrences that, even after the fact, after the scenario has been unveiled, after the film has been screened and its final twists are known, continue to seem unthinkable, incalculable.

We knew nearly everything about Nazism. We had read *Mein Kampf.* We had heard Hitler. But few were those who understood what he meant when he compared himself to Siegfried waking the Valkyrie imprisoned by the shadowy Nibelungen. Few were those who, having heard representatives of the Polish resistance describing, as early as 1942, the transfer of thousands of Jews to Auschwitz "for the sole purpose of immediately exterminating them in gas chambers," did any better than US Supreme Court Justice Felix Frankfurter after listening to Jan Karski: "I do not think that you 'lied,'" Frankfurter said, "but I cannot believe you." And even today, when we seem to know all there is to know about that extermination and its industrial mechanics, it remains within history's heart like an unbreakable kernel of night, as Primo Levi, Imre Kertész, and Elie Wiesel observed time and again.

We knew all there was to know about Putin's denial of the Ukrainian identity. One had only to listen to his speeches over the years to the Valdai Discussion Club to grasp the obsessive hate he bore for the West, the resentment he harbored for valiant Ukraine, and the resemblance, feature by feature, between his *Greater Russia* and Hitlerian *Lebensraum*. One had only to open one's eyes to see that the Kremlin, in a movement of troops not seen since the implosion of the USSR, was massing a combat-ready force of 300,000 on the Donbas border. It was a short step to conclude that he was going to move into action and throw himself into this insane enterprise, but it was a step that staggered the imagination and passed over the heads of most intelligence agencies. And, years later, though the step had indeed been taken, and though I had debated Putin's ideologist, Aleksandr Dugin, in Amsterdam on September 20, 2019, and heard him recite the entire catalogue of racist, anti-Semitic, and pro-Islamist insanities that are the essential ingredients of the Eurasian ideology, there is something enigmatic, something that defies logic and understanding, in the decision Putin made on February 24, 2022, to launch the "special operation" to take all of Ukraine.

The same is true of the sudden and sustained killing spree carried out on October 7 by the death squads of Hamas.

Many have wondered how the Mossad could have been fooled to such an extent as to miss the lead up to what would be the worst massacre of Jews since the Holocaust.

The reality is that there were signs here and there.

And the truth is that all of the world's intelligence services had the means to detect those signs.

A BBC analysis dated November 27, 2023, describes how the terrorists, as early as 2020, engaged in training sessions at nine different sites in the Gaza Strip just a few hundred meters from the security barrier.

On some such occasions, they would rehearse a rocket attack or the boarding of a dummy tank flying the Israeli flag.

On another, they simulated the "liberation" of the kibbutzim of Be'eri and Kfar Aza, describing the process on a dedicated Telegram channel.

One of the objects of these exercises was an attack on a full-scale military base, a model of which IDF soldiers would later find ten meters underground.

On yet another occasion, drones were used in a localization exercise; the drones were spotted by an IDF border protection unit, which reported the incursion up the chain of command, triggering reprisals in April 2023.

And, on September 12, twenty-five days before the fateful day, a final rehearsal seems to have taken place, also visible on a Telegram channel, in which terrorists filmed themselves assaulting mock buildings, landing on a mock beach, and entering houses similar to those assaulted on October 7.

As all this went on under the agencies' noses, they saw Yahya Sinwar, Hamas's military chief and organizer of the carnage, managing Gaza.

They saw him negotiating with the Israelis day to day for an easing of the blockade, as a result of which he received materials that could be used to manufacture weapons and build tunnels.

Each month, he quietly received from the hands of the ambassador of Qatar the millions of dollars needed to pay civil servants.

He presided over the construction of beaches (yes, there were beaches in Gaza, thanks in good part to the work of EcoPeace, an organization created by Israeli, Jordanian, and Palestinian ecologists expert in the cleaning of sea waters).

He encouraged the construction of five-star hotels (yes, there were five-star hotels in Gaza—including the luxurious Al-Mashtal Hotel belonging to the Marriott chain).

Everyone was delighted that Sinwar allowed universities, restaurants, riding clubs, and villas to flourish, and these were no secret on Gazan social networks.

He seemed to have mellowed.

This criminal, whom Israel sentenced four times to life in prison but who was released in 2008 after being treated for brain cancer by Israeli surgeons, was passing for a pragmatic moderate.

We watched him get serious enough during the Covid pandemic to make Gaza a model of public health, with an 8:00 p.m. curfew and a three-week quarantine for foreign visitors.

He gave press conferences.

He received foreign dignitaries.

As late as May 2021, after two weeks of one of those wars that he would inflict on Israel, as if routinely, he permitted himself, on the first day of a ceasefire that he had wisely negotiated, the luxury of a walk, out in the open, through the ruins of a neighborhood in Gaza City, during which he took selfies like a calm guy who has nothing to fear from the IDF because the IDF believes he has become a reasonable partner.

All of which is to say that we saw without really seeing or believing what we saw.

No one supposed that the same man was, at that same moment, preparing the most brutal and sophisticated attack in Israel's history.

And the very fact that these preparations were taking place as they were—practically out in the open—led our lazy imaginations to chalk them up to minor morale-boosting operations to keep the troops busy. But few, very few, felt the evil wind rising.

To explain this incredible failure, there is no need to wheel out the heavy artillery of conspiracy theories, such as diabolical agencies knowingly allowing the attack to come in the hope of doing away once and for all with a sworn enemy.

No need to point a finger at a guilty party—that is, a scapegoat who, when the right time comes, will be assigned full responsibility for the disaster, such as the global urban legend that has Israel being complicit with Hamas and purposely allowing its influence to grow.

The truth is both simpler and scarier.

That truth is the eternal propensity of democracies, when faced with unthinkable barbarity, to know without believing, to possess the data without drawing conclusions.

It is the logic of Edgar Allan Poe's purloined letter, lying on the table with scarcely a wrinkle but so obvious that no one takes any notice; it is, in other words, hidden in plain sight.

This is the paradox, theorized by the structuralist masters, of an epoch defined less by what it sees than by what the structure of its knowledge and the framework of its expectations render invisible.

And it is the second characteristic of those Events that reverse the dials of history. They are so distant from our habitual range of view that we do not see them emerge; they are so foreign to what a mind might conceive that they may as well be written in an unknown language; they are aberrant and fantastic, irreducible, even after the fact, to their context; a philosopher might say that they are one of the names of the impossible or that, even if they are of course not without a cause, they are larger than any cause, there is more substance in their effect than in their cause, and, for this reason, they have a dark and lasting force.

Which leads to the last and probably most important property of an Event.

It is a rending not of the veil of the Temple, as in the gospels celebrating a Nativity recurring as I write these lines during the Christmas season, but of the veil of Time itself.

It is a breach, a tear—a severing of the very flow of days and things.

And, for this reason, it breaks history in two.

It has no past, but it has a future.

It has no genesis, but it has an aftermath.

And though it is illogical, abusive, monstrous, though no principle of reason is sufficient to explain or produce it—in short, though it is not wholly of this world—it is of the world that comes after and helps make it.

It has, as French philosopher and psychoanalyst Jacques Lacan said, *a future*.

The Hamas killers themselves certainly have no future.

The butchers who will somehow manage to elude the Israelis, who are determined to destroy them in Gaza and to hunt them down wherever they may go, will end up before an international criminal court.

They may feign ignorance of this (as the leaders of the infernal columns of October 7 keep doing from down in their tunnels, where they pretend to be "negotiating").

They may continue to promote themselves in vile communiqués in which they acknowledge "errors" in how the attack was managed.

They may pretend to care about the fate of the Palestinians whom they condemned to death in cold blood.

They may act as if there could still be a life for them after so many deaths; they may display the degree of obstinacy, hardened cynicism, and criminality that allows their political leaders to continue strutting around, from Cairo to Doha, on the international stage; they may feed on the ashes of their own dead in the hope of maintaining their hold on the living whom they have taken hostage and transformed into human shields; all of that will merely render them fit to be raised onto the highest step of the podium of infamy, if such a thing existed.

No.

The Event of October 7 has a future because these consummate criminals, undeserving of a seat at any sort of negotiation table, have overturned the table.

They have turned the tables of a history that, confounding the Young Hegelians who idolize a form of globalization where all was to be for the best in the best of all possible worlds and where an army of little hands was working in the background for civil and international peace, has set itself back in motion.

It is no longer History with a capital "H" of course.

And Reason in Hegel's History has been succeeded by an unreason that no longer bothers to justify itself.

But these grim men have nevertheless changed, or helped change, the parameters of the world's cartography, its look and feel, and our new reality.

And they did it by producing three upheavals.

We will have to judge whether we are dealing with earthquakes that will leave us with brand new configurations—or whether, emerging from a trap door inadvertently opened in a cloud not of dust but of blood, we are facing the revelation, in the heat of the Event, of a colony of germs that were already present in the sewers not only of Gaza, but of the world.

3

Amalek's Bath

THE FIRST OF THESE UPHEAVALS targets the Jewish soul—and goes straight to the heart.

This is not the first time Israel has been forced into war.

Nor the first time it has been attacked on so many fronts: Gaza, Hezbollah, jihadist groups on the West Bank, Iran, the Houthis of Yemen, Syria, and the Shiite militias in Iraq.

So what's different?

Was it the stupefying effect created by the new scenario?

The number of dead?

The number of hostages, whose cause is sacred in Israel?

Was it the feeling of being caught in the trap of two imperatives that, for the first time in Jewish history, seemed tragically contradictory: eliminating Hamas *and* freeing the hostages; tracking the fighters through their maze of tunnels *and* looking for the children, women, and men whom the master blackmailers were holding at gunpoint, treating as bargaining chips, and whom they would not hesitate to execute when the Israeli commandos approached and the chips were suddenly worthless in the market of life and death; in short, obeying Maimonides's commandment in the *Mishneh Torah* that the freeing of captives is among the most holy of the *mitzvot*, a sacred duty, a mission one cannot shirk without "violating seven commandments of the Torah," *and* disarming a terrorist army whose paramount weapon is those same captives?

Was it the Nova rave and the 364 teenagers who had come to Re'im to celebrate and were picked off like rabbits?

Or was it the abrupt piercing of the Jewish state's armor of invulnerability?

For Israel, it was a dizzying moment.

But for Jews in the rest of the world, it was a hellish plunge into an unknown abyss.

France's Jews had experienced the barbaric murder of Ilan Halimi in 2006, when the young man was kidnapped, abducted for twenty-four days, tortured, and killed by a gang fueled by anti-Semitism.

They witnessed the postmortem denial of justice dealt to Ilan's namesake, Sarah Halimi, an elderly woman who had been murdered and defenestrated in 2017. Her killer was acquitted due to cannabis use, regardless of the anti-Semitic nature of the crime; the injustice was scandalous, and I responded by suggesting a new law enabling prosecution in these cases be created and named for her.

The massacre of six in Toulouse in 2012, the killings of hostages in the Hyper Cacher kosher market in Paris in 2015, and the 2018 fatal stabbing of Holocaust survivor Mireille Knoll in her home had revealed evidence of something that even the 1930s had avoided: the France of the Declaration of the Rights of Man and of Voltaire was turning into a country where one could die from being Jewish.

Wearers of the kippa in Marseille, Lyon, and Avignon were living in fear.

Jewish journalists and intellectuals, whether Jews by belief, tradition, or affirmation, were living under police protection.

But even if most of them stood firm, even if they knew that they had built France and that there was no question of allowing it to come apart by their departure, even if they said loud and clear that it would be a terrible moral debacle to cede the country of Chrétien de Troyes, Rashi, Racine, and Marcel Proust to illiterates who despised them only because they were the flower of France, another thought always made it a bit easier to stay put: the idea of an Israel of plenty that, with its deserts transformed into orange groves, its white stone glowing under a steady bright sun, its hyperactive democracy no less vibrant for the lack of a constitution, and its invulnerable army, to date undefeated, was there as insurance against the worst.

Now, we were seeing and feeling that insurance policy slipping away.

Now, the refuge was becoming a trap, and the place that was the symbol of "never again!" was where "again" had come down like a bolt of lightning.

Now, the European nightmare of the philosopher Emmanuel Levinas, the prospect he raised in *Proper Names* of "an icy wind" blowing through the rooms of well-to-do Jews in Paris and Berlin, pulling down the "drapes and tapestries" passed down through the generations, and sweeping away all the "small splendors" of every Jew, their lives transformed into so much tinsel to be seized by the "howling" of a "pitiless mob." And that vision of horror was now becoming possible in Israel and, from Israel, after gathering new energy and inspiration, was returning to Europe, to the United States, everywhere.

For my part, I do not believe that Israel was really threatened with actual annihilation.

I noted the relative moderation with which the Arab states that signed the Abraham Accords, mindful of their long-term interests, reacted to all this.

But there is geopolitics and there is the other geography, that of dreams, fears, and imagination.

And in that other space, the geosymbolic space that is no less influential in determining how people stand in the world, the situation is incontrovertible.

October 7 marks the alignment, for the worse, of Israel with the diaspora.

The two paths of Judaism are now on the same footing and are intersecting.

And the material and spiritual Jewish strength that is essential to the survival of real Jews, as I argued in *The Genius of Judaism*, has revealed its hidden weakness.

There is nowhere in the world where Jews are safe; that is the message.

No land on this planet is a shelter for Jews; that is what the Event of October 7 proclaims.

Never and nowhere will it be possible to say that Jews can live in the world the way the French live in France, the English in England, and the Americans in America—and that will be true until the end of time: such is the obvious truth.

It is the revenge of Amalek, of the oldest enemy of the Jewish people, the one who appeared as soon as the Jews left Egypt and were camped in the Sinai Desert. Now he has come out of limbo to bang on our doors and drum in our ears.

Amalek embodies the radical negationism that, from avatar to avatar since the time of Haman, has inspired the same plans for a "final solution," with Hitler having been its most recent face.

Amalek is the terrifying being that has no other attributes or will than the inborn, radical, and eternal hate that he bears for Jews.

Since there have been Jews, Amalek's name has been enough to cause fear and trembling among the pious—and even the not so pious!

So it's Amalek who comes to remind us that he will always be with us, like bad fate.

Amalek, too, knew that he would lose the war.

He was not unaware that, by plunging into the bubbling tub of the Jewish people, he would be scalded.

In this sense, he was the patron saint of the suicidal men of Hamas who throw themselves onto the hot walls of fortress Israel knowing full well that this is where they will remain.

But Amalek knew that, in so doing, he would cool down the bathwater and tarnish the image, prestige, and radiance of Israel.

And that is where we are, muse the Jews of October 7.

We stand precisely at the point where lively, bright, virgin Israel feels its splendor cooling and dimming.

And whether we are secular or mystic, modern or observant, whether we are Yiddish-speaking Hasidim from Williamsburg, freshmen at MIT or the Sorbonne,

Californians or New Yorkers, we all find ourselves thrown into the situation of our elders. We had hoped to escape it. But here it is.

4

Radical Evil

THE SECOND UPHEAVAL UNDERMINED universal consciousness.

Today, there is no question more pressing for humanity than that of the evil that one man can do to another.

The question has been off the West's radar for a long time now, having been methodically banished.

The banishment was the work of religions teaching that evil will be redeemed and that we must not settle for the idea that the world is a vale of tears.

It was the work of philosophy, the history of which can be read as an effort to find the right perspective from which—if you can just work yourself into that point of view—evil seems like a simulacrum (Plato), an optical illusion (Descartes), the limited view of a monad closed off from contemplation of the whole (Leibniz), a moment in a dialectic working toward transfiguration of the pile of petty miseries that we mistake for real history (Hegel).

Then came the moderns who, despite having been exposed to two world wars one on top of the other, competed to convince us that evil was a thing of the past. There were some veterans of the first war who invented the fiction of a socialism that would overcome the contradictions causing man's misery. There were others, survivors of the second war, who believed in a happy tomorrow where we would absorb the lessons of the catastrophe that had almost destroyed Europe and the world. And still others who applied the term "the end of history" to a cool and peaceful world in which globalized capitalism would allow everyone to adjust their needs and desires to those of their neighbors. According to that school of thought, evil was transformed into an illness and politics into a clinic.

Though apparently charming, this transformation turned out to be a veritable nightmare that I have decried since publishing *Barbarism with a Human Face* in 1977. And its epitome was recently reached when the world's fortunate convinced its wretched to confine themselves against a virus described as a common enemy, pushing into the background the evil that man inflicts on man.

Well, of course, it was an illusion.

For my own part, I never bought any of that nonsense.

But when, from Bangladesh to Rwanda and Darfur, new genocides belied the fable of "never again," we would say the events were far away and not our problem.

When, in Angola, Burundi, Somalia, or Afghanistan, in all the "forgotten wars" that I have spent a good part of my life chronicling, crime reigned supreme and plunged humanity into the "manure fire" portrayed by René Char (the French Resistance's "Captain Alexandre"), the vulgar Hegelianism that served as the litany of our era responded: these events remain peripheral, epiphenomenal, the fringes of an empire in the final phases of coming together and tolerating minor convulsions in its outlying provinces.

And when the earth burned in Bosnia or Algeria, when in 2014, Russia launched and then, in 2022, accelerated its invasion of Ukraine, setting it aflame, skillful and shameful dialecticians could still be found putting themselves in the shoes of the pyromaniacs and seeing in these arrythmias the last false notes of a concert of nations struggling to emerge.

Then came October 7.

Maybe the key point is that the event involved Israel, a country unlike all the others, one where nothing that has happened since the exodus from Egypt is viewed with indifference to the rest of the world's nations—usually for the worse, though sometimes for the better.

Maybe it is because the Islamists, having developed in Raqqa and Mosul the unprecedented practice of filming their deeds, communicated immediately on their social networks, proud of the severed heads, the skewered mothers, the tortured fathers.

Maybe, conversely, it's the deeply Jewish modesty that, echoing the Sinaitic proscription against idolatry or creating images of the unimaginable, prevented the Israelis from distributing those videos, paradoxically making the images all the sharper.

Maybe it's the courage of the survivors who, to quote the last sentence of Julien Gracq's 1938 gothic novel *The Castle of Argol*, felt the "the icy flash of a knife" slide between their shoulders "like a handful of snow," and by chance or by a miracle of bravery, escaped the slaughter and immediately told their full story to those who arrived on the scene. They would not be listened to for long. But in the narrow window accorded them by the global Spectacle, they offered poignant accounts that, ever so briefly, made their way into the minds of the world.

There was the media, all of it, including outlets not inclined to sympathize with Israel, whose talents seemed to have been enhanced by the general amazement. They will soon, of course, do their best to erase the event. But before that, they sent out their best sleuths to get the story and document its horrors. I am thinking in particular of the *New York Times*'s long investigation, which described a woman being pulled behind a pickup like an animal to the slaughter and, on the way, being raped by five men before being finished off with a knife. Another who, after being raped, had dozens of nails driven into her groin and thighs for fun. Two others killed by bullets shot into the vagina. Still another whose breasts were slashed by one man while another penetrated her. And another whose face was cut up before she was decapitated.

There was the number of children killed (thirty-five) and the universal scandal, in Kfar Aza as in Gaza, over the harm done to the innocent.

Among the children were two babies, one machine gunned (Mila Cohen), the other kidnapped (Kfir Bibas). Children who could hardly speak…. Human beings human only in body and for that reason perhaps more human than those fully formed…. Naked creatures with no experience of the violence, contempt, stupidity, pride, vanity, treachery, and meanness of other human beings…. These creatures purely pure, purely innocent, blank pages waiting for life to fill them in, these young beings about whom I have come to think that the respect we pay them is one of the things that remains, in the new human crowd, of the memory of a God whom we have often made a pure figure of the mind—are they not, these children, the irrefutable proof of the intolerable cruelty of Hamas?

The fact is that what we had not wanted to see in Algeria when the emirs were cutting babies into slices and the philosopher André Glucksmann and I were nearly the only ones howling in rage; what we had refused to see in Syria when a dictator ordered his opponents dissolved in acid baths, their wives raped in front of their parents, and their children exposed to banned chemical weapons; what I had filmed in Nigeria, where Boko Haram and Fulani militants were hacking up Christians with machetes—we had all of that recorded right before our eyes in Israel. All of the colorful masks with which assassins customarily disguise themselves fell from the faces of these "liberators" as they phoned their families holding a bloody pulp at arm's length, crowing, "Mom, your son is a hero! I killed ten... ten with my own hands...." All the strategies of avoidance and containment, all the tricks of conscience, all the conjuring rhetoric that we had been deploying for twenty, fifty, eighty years or more—all of it was pulverized by the Event.

Evil was there.

Pure evil, plain-faced, gratuitous, senseless.

Evil for nothing and for no reason; evil raw and unadorned.

Evil having neither power as its motive, nor pain as its memory, nor *Lebensraum* or a will to conquer as its obsession. Evil untethered to a war between ethnicities, nations, or ideologies.

Evil, true evil, that of the empty railway cars of Auschwitz, the repopulated rice paddies of Cambodia, and the Armenians forcibly marched to their deaths in the desert of Deir ez-Zor.

The Beast, the one from our beginnings, as it appeared at the twilight of the sixth day, just hours before man's introduction into the Garden of Eden.

The Serpent whose essence has not changed over time and who lurks in the fibers of man.

Immediate, unmediated, tautological evil; evil driven by no other passion than the passion for itself; the evil of man devouring man.

More than the Israeli or Jewish soul was murdered here; it was our common conscience.

More than a monstrous pogrom that sent Jewish memory back eighty years, it was another crack in the fragile veneer of civilization that had, for years, been tenuously holding the world *just* above the moral abyss that, from atrocity to atrocity, history permits us to glimpse from afar.

And for a short moment, too short, but long enough to be marked as a black day on the calendar of those who had sworn to remember—the world was gripped by a brutal, ravaging, stunning fear at seeing the Beast unchained and, with its muzzle bared, hungry for Jewish flesh—which is to say, human flesh.

After such a thing, we can always try to drown it in verbiage, bad faith, and an ocean of tweets.

We can, and already have, launched into a frantic yet methodical rewriting of the whole sequence of events.

But everyone saw, everyone knew, everyone recognized the landscape of a hell covered, as in Dante's *Inferno*, in blood, fire, and iron.

Evil was there, and it galloped over the patch of ground that the devil had given it.

Evil was back, resounding, insatiable, in a devasted landscape where the light revealed only nothingness.

Radical evil.

5

The Empire of Hamas

AND THEN, THE THIRD UPHEAVAL.

For an instant the world saw what it did not want to see.

And what it saw was a planet that froze briefly before beginning to turn again—but now turning on new bearings.

In 2018, I wrote a book entitled *The Empire and the Five Kings*. The title was an allusion to the Biblical story of the five kings whom Abraham fought to save his nephew, Lot.

In that book, I described an empire consisting of Europe, its American outgrowth, and others in the rest of the world that have faith in the Western Enlightenment.

I argued that this empire, which I called the "Global West," is contracting nearly everywhere, both in people's minds and geographically.

I showed how the space left vacant by the empire's retreat was creating opportunities for five new kings, five potentates, who ruled over countries that had once been the centers for powerful empires and aspired to become so again.

My thesis was that these five kings—Russia, China, the Iran of the ayatollahs, neo-Ottoman Turkey, and the Arab countries prone to jihadism—were ready to forgo their ancient enmities if that were the price of reviving the glory of Peter the Great, the Qing and Ming dynasties, the Ottoman viziers, the shahs of Persia, or the Umayyad and Abbasid sultans.

The book was written in the context of the war against the Islamic State, the role of the Kurds in that war, and then, at the moment of the battle of Kirkuk—which in my eyes was the equivalent of the ancient battles that put an end to the hegemony of Sparta, Athens, or Macedonia—how casually their western allies abandoned them once they had served their purpose.

The book's thesis was confirmed by the subsequent war against Ukraine, where we saw the same five— joined by a North Korea drunk on its own power—in coalition against a Global West that sometimes seemed to be pulling itself together while, at other times, looking like a heavy-footed giant with a head full of clay, a disconcerting mix of authority and restraint, extreme power and inexplicable cowardice.

But now we were seeing the five picking up where they left off, consolidating their alliance, and submitting us all to a new test, this time on the Israeli front.

What was true in the Kurdish and Ukrainian cases is proving true in the case of Hamas—but in reverse, and from the dark side of the world.

And it is around this minuscule terror state, this barbarous Lilliput, about which the big five had previously cared so little, that the dark planets realign and the new world takes shape.

The big difference is that the United States does not seem to be the same stumbling, dazed, declining empire ready to abdicate its throne.

I say "seem" because America still shows a reluctance to fully flex its muscles, to assert its creed and values. It moves ahead and retracts, takes a step toward Israel and pulls back. And nothing can be taken for granted as the vertiginous unknown looms with the upcoming presidential election.

But regardless of the current or future US position, what is sure is that the revisionist kingdoms were there for October 7 and that we found all five of them as fiery as ever and ready to get back in the game.

That appeared immediately among the Sunni powers who are the natural allies of Hamas. There was dancing in Kabul; in Islamabad, cries that bin Laden had been avenged; in Qatar, it occurred to no one to disturb Ismail Haniyeh and his retinue who were still, at least until further notice, Hamas's senior leaders; at most, they were asked—politely and after days of talks—to close their luxurious villas and leave for a well-deserved vacation in Algeria.

It was clear with respect to Turkish president Erdogan, the grand master of the confraternity of the Muslim Brotherhood, of which Hamas is the avant-garde. He did not lose a minute before resolving the ambiguities that previous signs of rapprochement with Jerusalem, linked with his nation's gas interests, might have generated. On October 24, Erdogan declared that "Hamas [was] not a terrorist organization" but rather "a group of mujahideen who are defending their land." We saw him, his neck wrapped in a Palestinian keffiyeh, at a huge rally at the old Atatürk Airport in Istanbul, where he informed the "whole world" that Israel is committing unpardonable "war crimes." Then, on December 27, this great humanist who has yet, a century after the fact, to acknowledge the Armenian genocide and is still fueling the same hatred today in Nagorno-Karabakh, compared Bibi Netanyahu to Hitler and the Palestinian refugee camps to the Nazi death camps. Nor did Turkey's membership in NATO or its economic reliance on the United States dissuade him from announcing on January 14, 2024 that his government possessed solid proof of Israel's genocidal activities in Gaza and would furnish them forthwith to the International Court of Justice, which was then in the process of examining and ultimately dismissing the formal complaint to this effect that had been filed by South Africa.

Iran began with denial. And perhaps remembering the good old days of the "nuclear agreement" with Teheran worked out by President Obama and his vice president, Joe Biden, the American administration went out on a limb to confirm, in the early hours, that there was no "proof" of Iran's "direct" involvement in the attack. But we learned quickly enough, through Iran's official press agency, that a meeting had taken place in Doha on October 14 between Ismail Haniyeh, who had not yet departed for Algeria, and the Iranian minister of foreign affairs, Hossein Amir-Abdolla-hian. This was followed on October 26 by a meeting in Moscow between Iranian vice president Ali Bagheri and another delegation of the terrorist organization, this one of lower rank. And then another meeting in Teheran, probably on November 6, between Haniyeh and the Supreme Leader himself, Ayatollah Ali Khamenei.

We quickly learned that there had been others, in August and September, well before the attack. We also learned that, according to what the *Wall Street Journal* described as "highly placed sources within

Hezbollah and Hamas," representatives of the Revolutionary Guard and, on least two occasions, Minister Abdollahian himself had reportedly helped during these meetings to "set up" the operation, "ironed out the details," and, on October 2 in Beirut, given it the "green light."

For those still in doubt, the regime's minister of culture, Ezzatollah Zarghami, a retired general of the IRGC, gave the story the fillip it lacked. In an interview released by the semi-official Mehr News Agency, Zarghami affirmed that he was "afraid of no one" and willingly admitted that his country had delivered to Hamas a quantity of Fajr-3 ballistic missiles of the type that had been used to strike Israel. So, "Iran outside Iran" must be added to complete the picture. Hezbollah's launches over the northern border of the Jewish state. The Shiite militias in Iraq ramping up attacks on American positions in Syrian and Iraqi Kurdistan and threatening Israel. And last but not least, the Houthis in Yemen—equipped with an arsenal of drones, medium-range ballistic missiles, and anti-ship missiles unparalleled in the region, and supported by a Revolutionary Guard spy vessel that makes little secret of guiding the attacks—who were harassing ships in the Red Sea they deemed to have any link with the "Zionist entity."

Was China testing, as in Ukraine, the adversary's capacity for resistance in the great confrontation to come? Was it pondering "Thucydides' Trap," that fateful moment when, according to the ancient Greek historian (as recounted by American professor Graham Allison), a waning power (yesterday, Athens, today, the United States) commits the fatal error of responding with force against the rising power (then, Sparta, now, China)? Or, conversely, was it running the risk of falling into what I dubbed Herodotus' Trap in *The Empire and the Five Kings*, in homage to the great historian of the Greco-Persian wars and his account of the ultimate victory of democracy over tyranny? Was China thinking of moving into Taiwan, and did it want to see whether America's wound might be widening, hastening the decline of its influence?

Whatever the reason, Chinese premier Xi Jinping abandoned his customary restraint, as he had with Ukraine. While stifling Tibet and annihilating the Muslim Uighurs, he refrained from condemning Hamas, refused to label it a terrorist organization, let flourish on Chinese television and Weibo fake news of the type, "Jews represent just 3% of the American population but control 70% of its wealth," and took the lead in the anti-Israel crusade that was gathering force among the BRIC nations.

But the icing on the cake was Putin. Over the years, he found useful idiots to serve up the edifying story of little Vladimir, poor and lost, raised by a Jewish family to which he remained attached and owed the remnants of his philo-Semitism. But the admirer of Czar Nicholas I in him remembered that Russia, at the height of its power, massacred tens of millions of Russians, persecuted hundreds of thousands of Jews, and planned, during the waning days of Stalinism, to do their fair share in bringing about the "final solution of the Jewish problem."

And above all, the KGB man of a thousand ruses, the crowned seditionist who has thrived only through plots, assassinations, pawns advanced, pawns sacrificed, and power gained with guns and bribes, the postmodern Mad Max who has replaced the motorcycles of the apocalypse with tanks and hypersonic missiles and likes being blessed by Rolex popes who wear their cowls the way Attila wore his caps—*that* Putin was aware of the benefits he stood to gain from this new Middle Eastern war, which was drawing the world's attention away from the heinous crimes he was committing in Ukraine.

So, he unleashed his pack, allowed his henchmen to revive the old national anti-Semitism and to warn Israelis of Russian origin that they would not be welcome when they flee their beloved "refuge" just ahead of the bombs. He did not deny that the Hamas leaders had two sessions with Russian Foreign Minister Sergey Lavrov (in September 2022 and March 2023), whose announced purpose was to "weaken the West," or that said leaders later returned to Moscow to meet with Iranian officials. He could not hide the fact that the red carpet was rolled out for them in the days following October 7, or that the Kremlin had still not condemned the massacre.

The circle is nearly complete.

It is almost the same picture, but worse, that we watched take shape at the time of the war against the Kurds and again with the war against Ukraine—which, incidentally, continued unabated in a world where everything was suddenly splitting in two: the media's focus, the attention of foreign ministries, and even military aid, which some political leaders, expecting Trump to return to power and taking advantage of the general confusion, would like to let fall by the wayside.

Could it be said that this upheaval is not really an upheaval this time around since it is just the same old song?

Is it the fortress Europe (and America) emitting its endless but familiar supply of collaborators and appeasers? Yes and no.

It is as if tectonic plates had been rubbing together, sliding, overlapping, and separating before suddenly interlocking in a new pattern.

And for today's observers, the current scene is a panorama where everything seems perfectly in place.

Hamas is no longer Hamas but, instead, the sword and toy of a counter-empire wherein the protagonists of the preceding wars have come together permanently.

And Israel, reciprocally, is a little more than just Israel. It carries the message, even if unknowingly, of the Uighurs of China, the intrepid bloggers of the Arab autocracies, the proponents of the Armenian cause in Istanbul who detest Erdogan and his fables of the Grand Turk, the strong souls of Kurdistan, the Iranian insurgents who continue to cry "Woman, Life, Freedom," the opponents whom Putin deports, sends into internal exile, and assassinates—and also, perhaps in spite of themselves, the Palestinians in silent revolt against the Hamas dictatorship.

This has nothing to do with a war between West and East.

Nor with the "war of civilizations" that some, already lining up their legions, are hoping for.

Or maybe it does. But in that case, one of the civilizations is the fine *Internationale* of the friends of liberty, law, and the spirit of resistance, drawing its members from within the new and ancient empires alike. And the other is the civilization of tyrants and demagogues whose followers are recruited in the West no less than in the East or South.

The Maharal of Prague wrote in *Netzach Yisrael* that, in contrast to kingdoms and empires, which are extensive, Israel is a point, a single point, but what a point! The central and hidden point, secret and essential, upon which rests, in the terrible dramaturgy of history, a piece of human survival.

So there we have it. Israel is not a pawn, but a point.

It is the hearth that radiates a light and a language without which a part of humanity would be lost.

Israel exists in a kind of solitude, no doubt. A terrible solitude.

But to paraphrase Albert Camus, there are women and men, many women and many men, who would be very alone indeed without this solitary presence and who pray each morning and each evening, more or less secretly and silently, summoning whatever boldness their status as hostages of the five kings allows, for Israel to win its war against the empire of Hamas.

PART TWO

Negationism In Real Time

6

Events Can Be Erased

BUT A SECOND EVENT QUICKLY followed the first.

It was like a reply, a second strike, intensifying the first with muted but equally devastating violence.

And this second event defused, suppressed, and caused people to *forget* the scope of the first.

About the reality of the acts, there was obviously no doubt.

The assassins documented themselves and their heinous deeds using GoPro cameras affixed to their foreheads or the handlebars of their motorbikes.

And whereas Stalin kept trucks running so the sound of their engines would muffle the screams of those being tortured in Lubyanka; whereas the Nazis hid the evidence of extermination so that new waves of deportees being led to the gas chamber would believe, until the last minute, that they should line up quietly, fold their clothes neatly, and march toward the showers, the Hamas terrorists owned their crimes and posted them on TikTok.

In spite of this evidence, there were some cynical souls who came forward immediately after October 7 to say that they either saw nothing or did not believe what they had seen.

A new quarrel over images engulfed the conspiracy theorists of Europe and the United States. The dispute reminded me of the debate launched by filmmaker Jean-Luc Godard, decades after the Nazi defeat, over the absence of images of the gas chambers: "Images! Oh, images… They mean nothing, anyway, images… You can make them say what you want them to say!" Godard, Claude Lanzmann, and I almost made a film about the issue.

When a few accounts delivered in the heat of the moment by speakers full of emotion turned out to be shaky, hasty, or faulty, these were used to cast suspicion on the others. All the others. The eyewitness accounts of the shootings, the mutilations, the rapes, all to the tune of "Nothing, nothing at all, I saw nothing in Be'eri, nothing happened in Kfar Aza… All that is just lies, delirium, a put-up job…"

We watched as New York Congressman Jamaal Bowman publicly called into question whether Israeli women were really raped and then doubled down, calling the accusations "propaganda."

We watched as an adviser responsible for combatting violence against women in David Cameron's Foreign Office lent her support to a petition contesting the information in the article in the *New York Times.* Rapes? the petition asked (in effect). We still don't have proof. And even when we get it, there's nothing to show that the rapes were committed by Hamas and not by the Israeli army.

But shouldn't we give credence to the women's word? In the climate ushered in by the recognition of a woman's right to speak up, isn't the new norm that we must listen to the victim first and then confront the presumed rapist? Yes, of course. But not if the woman is Israeli. Not if she is one of the women of Kfar Aza who, having survived the beatings of October 7, are still shaking with fear when they testify, their voices cracked and their eyes dry from too much crying. The victims' word, said the petition, is a tool of "propaganda" in service of the "occupation," "genocide," and "ethnic cleansing."

Some militants, of course, stood against this obscenity. As a riposte, a strong hashtag appeared, #MeTooUnlessYoureAJew. But the fact is that the main feminist groups didn't rise up to support their Israeli sisters.

In France, we saw a young legislator from the left-wing populist party, *La France Insoumise*—France Unbowed—which, from its start, has bowed down to every tyrant it encountered, extend his party's streak in a particularly ugly fashion by telling an amused and captive audience in Tunis that the reports of the crimes of October 7 reminded him of an earlier event: "Yes, of course!" he exclaimed. "Crimes… rapes… doesn't this smell like Sabra and Shatila, in 1982? So, Israel!"

The leader of his party, Jean-Luc Mélenchon, was a little more prudent, but no less perverse. He abstained from condemning Hamas on October 7 and refused to characterize the killings and kidnappings as acts of terrorism. Instead, he saved his shots for an episode of madness three days later, when he accused his sworn enemies in the council of French Jewish organizations, who were then marching in the streets, of aligning themselves with the "far-right Israeli government" and preventing "France's solidarity with the desire for peace."

Mélenchon doubled down in the weeks that followed, becoming more expansive and feverish—all with a strange earnestness that reminded me of the time when, as a young socialist, he was pining over being unloved by François Mitterrand, scorned by comrades higher ranked than he in the Marxist circles that then occupied the high ground, and unable to muster the speculative sophistication that seemed to him the ultimate in political chic. At the time, we saw this two-bit radical who, to parody a phrase of André Gide's, had set himself up as a revolutionary the way one sets up as a hairdresser. We watched this Robespierre made up as Bertie Wooster and flexing the dialectic the way one might flex one's muscles, one minute urging economic sanctions against Israel on the basis of "experience of the struggles" of "South African comrades," the next, explaining pompously that labeling a group a "terrorist organization" was always "the result of a power relationship," so there was "no sense" in this "context" to "label Hamas as a terrorist entity," and the next, whining that he felt "abandoned by the Jews." His outbursts, interventions, and dreadful displays placed him squarely in the dirty tradition of leftist French anti-Semitism at the time of the Dreyfus affair.

His American analogues, the Democratic representatives of "the Squad," who likewise describe themselves as progressives despite having long ago said goodbye to the universalist humanism of the Enlightenment, took the same line. We saw Rep. Rashida Tlaib of Michigan declare her support for the "Palestinian resistance" and voice her disapproval of AIPAC, which she claimed had become a "threat to democracy." Rep. Jamaal Bowman, who later cast doubt on the rape allegations, released a statement on October 7 that, after denouncing the attack by Hamas, moved quickly to blame the Israeli "blockade of Gaza." And the Democratic Socialists of America, far from uttering any word of solidarity with victims of October 7, lent their support to an "All Out for Palestine" rally in New York on October 8, emphasizing its "solidarity with the Palestinian people and affirming their "right to resist 75 years of occupation and apartheid."

As for the 240 hostages who had seen their loved ones raped, beheaded, and gutted before being led like cattle into the wet tunnels of Khan Younis, there to be humiliated, beaten, starved, drugged, and raped— the so-called "progressives" of the Democratic Party quickly came to act as if they did not exist.

Meanwhile, except in Israel, where practically the entire country turned out each Saturday in a massive display of solidarity similar to that which had united them in opposition to Netanyahu's wildly unpopular judicial reforms, we saw no walls of names or faces to remind people and governments of their existence and to fight the silence that is the greatest danger in such situations.

When ordinary citizens took to posting the faces of kidnapped children in the neighborhoods of New York or Los Angeles, they were met with actions unprecedented in the history of street protests. No second sign was posted in reply. Nor (as in election campaigns) was it enough to cover the first with a competing one, which is dishonorable enough. No. The faces were torn down. We saw dutiful fathers, dignified women slashing, slicing, and stripping down the photos. And when others tried to intervene, we heard and saw the perpetrators fly into fits of rage and delirium, declaring, "I don't believe it... I'm not stupid... I don't believe it..."

The NGOs theoretically responsible for assisting those who had been kidnapped did not seem to believe it either. Like Amnesty International, they opted for vague jargon relegated to the bottom of their corporate sites, pumping up the organ of indignation only to denounce the Israeli response.

The Red Cross led the way by ignoring the captives, not deigning to visit them, half-heartedly inquiring about their welfare, and treating with unnecessary firmness a woman suffocating with pain who had only the Red Cross to turn to as she tried to get her aged mother essential life-saving medications. "Madam," the organization responded, in a tone more suitable for reproaching prison guards, "We do not do that."

No, that is not completely fair. The Red Cross did eventually inquire into the existence of the men, women, and children imprisoned in the tunnels of Gaza, sometimes under the very building that housed its own staff. But to do this, the organization required forty-eight days and the week-long cease-fire of November 24, during which Hamas blew hot and cold, released its prey in drips, and ceaselessly broke its own promises before returning to the agreement at the last minute, releasing 105 hostages.

In that case, the Red Cross answered, "Present."

It oversaw the observance of an indecent agreement in which one Israeli life was valued at three Palestinian lives, plus a handful of Thais who were released as a bonus.

But it was hard to tell what game these Red Cross representatives were playing when they emerged from their ethical discretion and appeared before the cameras. Were they escorting hostages whom they earlier said they knew nothing about? Or were they moved by the torturers whom we saw holding an adolescent's shoulders, helping an older woman out of a pickup, and presenting themselves to the world as polite, considerate young men honestly concerned with a "regional conflagration"? You might have mistaken them for camp counselors saying goodbye at the end of the summer!

In the end, none of these humanitarians objected to the semantic monstrosity inherent in the phrase "prisoner exchange," as if one could equate the criminals the Israelis were releasing, who had Jewish and Palestinian blood on their hands, with little Kfir Bibas, who spent his first birthday alone, without his family, without toys, and probably living in a cesspool. As I finish revising these pages, Kfir has spent 252 days in the hands of real-life monsters.

But in the race to make the hostages invisible, to put distance between ourselves and the deaths of October 7, and to relativize their torment, it was the United Nations that competed the hardest and took the first prize.

Of course, it had already been some time since the UN lost its moral dignity in the eyes of many militant defenders of human rights.

I remember Bosnia, where for four years running, the UN was unable to name the aggressors and stop the siege of Sarajevo.

I remember Rwanda, where it awaited the end of the killing before distinguishing the perpetrators from the victims.

Not to mention Ukraine, where, Russia's *droit de veto oblige*, it let itself fall into the trap of a terrorist Putin, expert in blackmail of every sort.

Then October 7 happened.

Right off the bat, Secretary General António Guterres set the tone by condemning only "the suffocating occupation" endured "for 56 years" by the people of Gaza, despite the fact that the occupation of Gaza had ended with a unilateral Israeli withdrawal in 2005.

Following this, the organization's entire apparatus, its agencies, commissions, and subcommissions, designed eighty years ago to embody Kant's cosmopolitan dream of universal peace, geared up to overwhelm Israel, denounce its response as disproportionate, and push the actual events of October 7 into the background.

Item: Francesca Albanese, special rapporteur for human rights in the occupied Palestinian territories. Passing over the massacre, she started by concentrating on the response, which she described as the "monstrosity of our century." On March 26, continuing her moral blindness, she had the nerve, in a report entitled "Anatomy of Genocide," to condemn Israel for perpetrating "acts of genocide" and declined to "examine those events" (i.e., October 7), as they were "beyond the geographic scope of her mandate."

Item: UN Women. This organization devoted, in principle, to defending women's rights around the world waited two months, like many feminist organizations in the United States, before denouncing the killings of women and grudgingly acknowledging the rapes committed, recorded, and celebrated by Hamas in the kibbutzim. Meanwhile, the organization did not object when its deputy head, Sarah Douglas, posed in front of a Palestinian flag and posted no less than 153 anti-Israel tweets.

When, finally, in March 2024, Pramila Patten, Special Representative of the Secretary-General on Sexual Violence, concluded after a lengthy fact-finding mission that "there [were] reasonable grounds to believe that conflict-related sexual violence—including rape and gang-rape—occurred" and that she was at last able to provide "clear and convincing information that sexual violence, including rape, sexualized torture, cruel, inhuman and degrading treatment, has been committed against captives," she would not release these findings without mentioning, in the same breath, her investigation into alleged sexual violence supposedly committed in the West Bank by Israeli forces against Palestinian women.

And when, on March 11, UN Women brought up this report before the Commission on the Status of Women, the group's executive director, Sima Bahous, stated that while it contained "horrific accounts of sexual violence against women and girls in the October 7 attack ... there are also harrowing testimonies of sexual violence by Israeli forces against Palestinian women in detention, house raids and checkpoints." Somehow she was able to utter the word "Israel" only in the context of unproven accusations, whereas Hamas, undeniably guilty of instructing its militants to rape and abuse Israeli women, was never mentioned by name.

And where did the report go once released? Nowhere. Its findings were buried under the bureaucratic mountain designed to lay Israel's suffering to rest.

Meanwhile, there were vehement protests within the UN itself against the rare individuals who rejected the absolution of the initial crime. Alice Wairimu Nderitu, Special Advisor on the Prevention of Genocide, was threatened with dismissal for daring to observe that a Jewish life is worth as much as a Palestinian one, and proposing to make the freeing of the hostages a precondition for negotiation. Cindy McCain, Executive Director of the World Food Programme (and wife of the former Arizona senator and presidential candidate), was lectured by her colleagues for agreeing to appear at a ceremony in Canada at which the John McCain Prize for Leadership in Public Service was to be awarded to an Israeli officer who, in their eyes, had suddenly become a Nazi.

And let us not forget UNRWA, the massive UN agency responsible for the bulk of humanitarian aid to the Palestinians. UNRWA deserves special mention because we now know it was a party to the crime. On January 6, 2024, an arsenal of grenade launchers was found in a dispensary in Khan Younis that the agency managed. A rocket manufacturing workshop was dismantled in the house next to its school in Beit Lahia, in northern Gaza. According to an oversight report on its educational programs and their conformity with UNESCO norms, some UNRWA instructors applauded the massacre. One called it a "splendid spectacle." Another, "the first real victory" in the "liberation" of Palestine. A third celebrated "an unforgettable and glorious morning."

Then, on January 27, the US Secretary of State himself announced the news that shocked the world:

a dozen UNRWA employees were personally involved in carrying out the pogrom. Funding was immediately halted by a number of countries, starting with the United States. But it was soon reinstated by France, Japan, Canada, Australia, Sweden, and others. And now UNRWA officials boldly deny, apparently without fear of contradiction, that there is any evidence of their members' participation in the attack.

All of this is a lot to consider.

Even in the eyes of someone long ago disabused of the ethics of the United Nations; even for those who witnessed Pakistan imposing an anti-blasphemy clause on the UN Human Rights Council or Iran chairing the social forum of the same council in Geneva; even for the jaded souls who did not burst out laughing at the announcement that Iran had assumed the presidency of the UN Conference on Disarmament in March 2024, or that Saudi Arabia had been elected to chair the Commission on the Status of Women for 2025; even for these, there was an almost unimaginable bias and double standard in the handling of October 7 and its aftermath.

And slowly but surely, with one thing leading to another, it was the Israeli hostages and victims who disappeared in the dark night of words, grievances, and lies that have descended on the planet.

It wasn't simply that Israel was being demonized; this is a tune we have heard many times.

Nor the fact that we had returned shamelessly to the time when UNESCO equated Zionism with racism.

No. What we saw was a world-historical Event being submerged, if not denied altogether.

The Event with a capital "E" that had struck the world's conscience like lightning was being relegated to the status of a contested detail in an ancient and intractable conflict in which both sides were equally at fault.

And it is the entire planet that attempted to forget that, several months, weeks, or days earlier, it had wavered on its axis, seen the gates of hell open, and heard the cry that, in the echo chamber of the centuries, is the sound of human terror in the face of absolute evil.

Rarely has negationism functioned so well and so quickly.

Rarely has the eraser applied to human filth, so dear to my dear Louis Aragon, worked so well.

And Europe, and the world, could now go quietly back to sleep.

7

Traps of Common Sense

IN THE METHODICAL DECONSTRUCTION of the Event, there were three themes, three canned phrases, that were all the more damaging for seeming to spring from common sense.

First, "Yes, but."

The indestructible, inextinguishable, eternal "Yes, but" so dear to professional excusers of evil.

Yes, of course, *the hostages*...began the official statement from the far left political party, France Unbowed, on the day of the assault. But they fell "within the context of the intensification of Israel's policy of occupation of Gaza and the West Bank." ("What occupation of Gaza?" lovers of truth might respond. Were they not aware that, after 2005 and the pullout of settlers ordered by Ariel Sharon, no Israeli presence remained? Had they not heard that, because the first thing the Palestinians did after the withdrawal was to burn down the synagogues and houses that the IDF left behind, there had not been the slightest Jewish presence in Gaza for the past seventeen years?)

Yes, *the pogrom*, people said.... It happened...but what about the horror of apartheid? Isn't Israel what South Africa was, an apartheid society? (One would like to remind these imbeciles that Israel is a country with two million Arabs, comprising 20 percent of the population, who enjoy the same economic, social, and civil rights as their Jewish fellow citizens; that there are more mayors and judges from this Arab minority than in any other democracy in the world; and that it is represented in the Knesset by several parties that permit themselves the luxury of detesting Zionism without letting that stop them from participating, whenever they can, in the formation of governing majorities.)

Yes, maybe so, parry the American and European defenders of identity politics...but the Jews belong to the suspect category of "privileged whites," whereas Hamas is a soldier (undisciplined, but a soldier all the same) in the great army of barefoot warriors battling what Jean Genet called "white rules." (I am embarrassed at having to respond to this, embarrassed at having to poke a finger into the gears of their reasoning, and embarrassed for those who take this position. Must they be reminded that Israel is home not only to Jews and Arabs, but also to Druze, Aramaeans, Bedouin, and Circassians? And among the Jews, aren't there Arab Jews, Ethiopian Jews, Asian Jews, Ukrainian Jews, and Russian Jews? Does anyone really need to be told that Israel is a multiethnic country, the only one in the region and one of the few in the world where this model has performed so well?)

Yes, but what about the Israeli far right, objected those who do not think and who reason only in terms of "escalation of violence".... Yes, but the distasteful ministers Itamar Ben-Gvir and Bezalel Smotrich who dream of razing Gaza to rubble and with whom Netanyahu has formed a shameful alliance so that he can cling to power.... (Come on! Beside the fact that these two ministers, though indeed a stain on Netanyahu's already smudged biography, do not amount to much in Israel's long and glorious history—let's be serious here! Can one imagine a Western neighbor of Giorgia Meloni's Italy using as a pretext her Mussolini-like leanings, her stance on migrants, or her failure to condemn a demonstration by a group of thugs performing fascist salutes—can one imagine a neighboring state, proto-state, or quasi-state launching a murderous assault against Italy resulting in an unimaginable number of deaths, proportional to the number killed by Hamas?)

Yes, but "the context," insist those on whom the attack was not inflicted, nodding sagely.

Ah, the context!

Once more, António Guterres set the tone by declaring that Hamas's attack, awful as it was, did not occur "in a vacuum" and had to be understood in the "context of Israel's occupation."

This same word—*context*—was sung in unison by France's politicians, the editorialists of the global South, and, in the United States, by the presidents of MIT, Harvard, and the University of Pennsylvania when they were asked by a panel of the House of Representatives whether calling for the murder of Jews constituted a violation of the rules in effect on their campuses.

Israel was defending itself.

Struck in the heart, Israel was attempting to neutralize the Nazis that had drawn its blood precisely to ensure that they could never do it again.

Cornered by the masters of the human shield technique, Israel was fighting a war that had just been declared against it. Unlike Erdogan ruthlessly liquidating Turkey's Kurds; Xi, China's Uighurs; and Putin, the Ukrainians and Chechens, Israel waged this war with respect for the laws of armed conflict. And all that its critics could muster in response, when they were not calling for a Palestine extending "from the river to the sea," was "yes, but."

There was a second argument that spread like a powder trail: the argument of the ceasefire.

Israel, I repeat, had just been assaulted as never before. Israel had suffered a terrorist attack akin to September 11 in the United States and the bombings of the Bataclan theater, the Charlie Hebdo newspaper, and the Hyper Cacher kosher market in Paris.

And just as the United States invaded Afghanistan, where Osama bin Laden and his gang had gone into hiding, just as France helped strike Raqqa and Mosul, where the attacks on French soil had been planned, Israel preemptively protected itself by going into Gaza.

But time having passed and the world having turned, it did so in a context where the parameters had completely changed:

1. The terrorist side had become bolder (with the jihadists targeting not a single theater or even two massive towers, but an entire country, one that they've vowed to destroy).

2. Hamas had assembled reinforcements and friends. (Unlike the Islamic State and Al Qaeda, it relies on the potent coalition of the Five Kings—Iran, Turkey, Russia, China, and the Islamist caliphs.)

3. The state of Israel was in a situation diametrically opposite to that of the United States and France. Both had faced an isolated adversary that had none of the international support Hamas now enjoyed. They also had the advantage of having formed numerous fraternal coalitions in which the military

and moral burdens of war were shared, whereas Israel has no choice but to act alone, relying solely on its own forces.

Now what happens?

What is the cry that arises, from day one, from all the embassies that have allowed Israel to go into combat alone?

Ceasefire!

Call an immediate halt to the fighting!

Gather around a table, quickly, and talk with Qatar, Egypt, Algeria—any old false witness and true friend of the terrorists capable of convincing them to gently agree to a pause, a truce, a cessation of hostilities!

The same idea crossed no one's mind when, on October 7, 2001, the United States launched its Afghan operation with the support of Britain and NATO.

I covered the battle of Mosul. I devoted a film to it. I documented the retaking of the Plain of Nineveh and the liberation of the historic city of the Prophet Jonah, a world heritage site. That liberation came at the cost of many civilian casualties and considerable destruction. But again, I do not recall any great democracy issuing a call for a ceasefire.

And if that were so—if no serious party considered imposing a ceasefire before Al Qaeda and ISIS could be defeated—it was for two reasons.

First, if we are talking about a true ceasefire, which is to say a humanitarian truce—then Israel has clearly taken the lead in this regard, proposing many deals that Hamas has systematically refused. Then again, such a truce can be risked only with great fear and trepidation, because when one is dealing with a terrorist organization, caliphate, or state, the likeliest effect of a ceasefire is to allow it time to regroup, replenish its weapons, reestablish its chain of command, and recommence its attack.

Second, the call for a ceasefire is merely a disguised manner of inviting compromise and peace with assassins. Did we ever propose peace with ISIS? Appeasement with Al Qaeda? Would it be reasonable to allow the terrorist organization, caliphate, or state not only to remake itself but also to claim victory, to be rewarded for its crimes, to show all over the world that its violence has paid off, and to watch as its image as an Arab David that has slain the Western Goliath grows and grows?

It is often said that jihadism is an idea, and that an idea cannot be killed with bombs.

In other words, if you neutralize one jihadist, ten more will spring up. Terrorists love death, the argument goes. They feed on the blood of others as well as their own, the result being that waging war against them fulfills their desires, confers on them the glory they had been lacking, and aids recruitment.

But this is factually untrue.

The defeat of Afghanistan in 2001, followed by bin Laden's death in 2011, did not eradicate Al Qaeda. But it tarnished its image, demolished its myth of invincibility, and discouraged many from joining the group that appeared to be on the losing side.

Destroying ISIS's command structures in Mosul, shrinking its operating territory to practically nothing, and in 2019, killing its leader Abu Bakr al-Baghdadi did not eliminate the last of the rag-tag soldiers who salute its flag, but the popularity, capacity for mobilization, and fighting force of the organization are far from what they were at its peak.

Incidentally, one must have a pretty low opinion of the people of the region to believe that they would be the only ones in the world to experience the defeat of a barbarous power as a new source of intoxication, an invitation to more martyrdom, and a call to shed more blood. Why would Palestine and the neighboring Arab states not react as Germany did after 1945, viewing military defeat as a deliverance, as German president Richard von Weizsäcker later said in an historic address?

But no. We are talking about Israel, and no one wants to entertain this hypothesis.

The subject is Israel, and 82 percent of the world's nations demand of it a restraint that they have never expected from any other nation that has been similarly attacked and threatened with extinction.

The subject is Israel, and we start from the principle (inconceivable anywhere else) either that it has no right of self-defense or that it must settle for a weakened Hamas—but a Hamas surviving, safe, and effectively victorious—at its borders.

And now, the third "common sense" argument: that of the "day after."

You read that right.

The Israelis had not finished with the "day of" before they were being asked to move on to the "day after."

They had not dried their tears, grieved, or recovered their hostages. There was a father who had buried his son but was still going from one office to the next to try to recover the boy's head, which he heard had been sold for $10,000 at a Gaza market. But already the Israelis were being asked about their plans, their intentions, their vision, what future they foresaw for a Palestinian people whose current leaders thought only of annihilating them.

In a matter of weeks, they had to organize the most complex war effort that a democratic nation has had to mount in decades. They had to manage the evacuation of two hundred thousand civilians in the south and, in the north, on the border with Hezbollah, shelter another hundred thousand. While they were organizing these movements, unprecedented in their history and colossal for the size of the country, Shiite militias from Syria set themselves in motion, and the towns of the West Bank, after dancing with joy, began to rumble with violent menace.

Faced with this existential challenge, the Israelis watched as experts, including retired generals, media commentators, and in France, Dominique de Villepin, a former prime minister pining for faded UN glory, crowded the television shows to deliver lazy and pretentious utterances in imitation of Clausewitz: "War is the continuation of politics by other means." No war is possible, said the experts, without a clear idea of the goal to be attained. Hamas is an idea and you cannot kill an idea with bombs, you can only make it stronger. So what's the goal here? What is the exit plan? What's in the head of these Israeli officers drunk on vengeance? It was obscene.

Well of course there will be a day after. There is always a day after, and the soldiers of the IDF know it as well as the professional commentators.

But what exactly are we talking about, and what precisely do these dispensers of wisdom have in mind when they say, with serious and subdued mien, that Israel has become a rudderless ship with no plan for the future?

Once again, there are two possibilities.

If the question is to decide who will administer Gaza, who will rebuild it, and how life will be restored to two million Gazans held hostage for seventeen years by unworthy leaders, then rest assured: Governments are holding talks. Think tanks are at work in Cairo, Abu Dhabi, and Riyadh. There are plans for an "Arab mandate." Other plans for a Palestinian Authority rebuilt from the ground up. And in Jerusalem itself, there is a plan that one may deem insufficient, hasty, and questionable, a plan that the prime minister himself had already challenged when his defense minister made it public in January 2024. But a plan was nonetheless proposed, one that is more concrete, precise, and responsible than any of the plans the Allies had in 1945 for postwar Germany and Japan. And it shows that the war cabinet had, if not a clear idea, then at least an inkling and a modicum of concern for what the Gaza of tomorrow should look like: Palestinian committees for administration; moderate Arab countries for reconstruction; technological monitoring of the border with Egypt; and no Israeli resettlement.

Alternatively, we may conclude that the architects of the Abraham Accords, starting with Israel, made a mistake in assuming that Palestinian claims to statehood were simply going to evaporate into the clouds of an emerging regional market. In which case, what we mean by "the day after" is the day of contrition when we tell the Palestinians, "You were forgotten, erased, entered into the losses column of history (even though history is never written without peoples). But it is never too late to make reparations, and that is what the international community is trying to force Israel to do!"

If that is the idea, then one should be very clear about it.

I, too, believe that history is not made without peoples.

I, too, believe (and wrote well before October 7) that the blind spot of the Abraham Accords was the Palestinian question.

And while I am dotting my i's, I have always been a proponent of a two-state solution—that is, a solution under which the rights of the Palestinians are recognized and granted, provided they do not deny the rights of the Israelis to recognition and basic security.

The first article I ever wrote, entitled "Zionisms (plural) in Palestine," was published shortly after the Six-Day War in the French journal of the International Committee of the Left for a Negotiated Peace in the Middle East. In it, I explained that the day the Palestinians accepted the existence of Israel and saw Zionism as the liberating movement that it is, it would be just to envision a Palestinian state.

I remember how happy I was when I believed that Yasser Arafat would accept Israel's offer at Camp David....

How gratified I felt by the Geneva Plan, of which I was one of the architects....

How excited by the idea of a "dry" peace that, in the face of the impasse at Oslo, I floated in 2002 in a speech in Tel Aviv. Make peace, not love, I said. Peace here and now, without waiting a month of Sundays for everyone to get to know and understand each other. Peace not at the conclusion, but at the start of the process. Because if you wait until the end, one of the partners can derail the train at the last minute.

Not to mention two additional episodes that I will one day recount in detail.

One involved Dominique de Villepin, who was then serving as a cabinet minister and was still a likable character with childlike, ever-changing, unpredictable enthusiasms. He always seemed to be following the cues of an inner director who never got his role right. Now an imperial general. Now a young ruffian wanting to take France out for a ride. Now a sudden fixation on literature. Now a straight-laced servant of the state practicing unflinching realpolitik.

During the season in question, de Villepin was experiencing the urge to think big for France, aided by a young and ardent adviser named Bruno le Maire (now France's minister of finance). President Bush had just proposed a "road map" that was supposed to revive the peace process. Well, the minister, already dry, a little mummified, but still not having donned the hostile mask of a right-wing Mélenchon that he would later wear, had little to contribute when it came to the topic of Israel besides a collection of stale clichés. But he wanted France to propose, in support of (or perhaps in competition with) the American initiative a "declaration of principles." He turned to me to write that declaration and then to recommend it to Israel and the Arab states. The project soon fell apart. But I remember my joy and enthusiasm at the prospect of taking the initiative.

The second episode was one of my many conversations with Ariel Sharon since our first meeting in Paris in 1979. My last. November 2005. Shortly before the double stroke from which he did not recover. "Do you know the size of Gaza?" he asked me that night in his office in Jerusalem while discussing his decision, controversial within his party, to pull out of the enclave. "Ten times larger than Dubai City. Ten! People don't realize that Israel is not that big. But Gaza is not as small as one thinks. And the Palestinians, if they're serious, will have the room they need to build ten Dubais, ten Singapores. And another thing..."

For a moment, he looked tired. His stout fighter's face clouded over with sadness. But he pulled himself together. His thick, oddly supple neck protruded like that of a porter unshouldering his burden. With a look that was suddenly faraway and in the tone of a man uttering his last wish, he told me, "As for Europe...

Europe has to know that we are withdrawing at the same time from the settlements in Judea and Samaria... By force, if need be... *Manu militari*... Because, for me, the two are linked..."

Yes. For this pioneer of Israel, this hawk, disengagement from Gaza was the prelude to the birth of a Palestinian state. Free Gaza was the miniature version, the prototype, of the state that he had come to see as necessary. As for me, when I left his office and found myself in the noisy streets of Jerusalem under a clear night sky, my heart was pounding with joy.

I bring up these memories now to show that few subjects have preoccupied me more in fifty years of activism.

But another reason I evoke them is because I want people to understand me when I say that now is not the time to trumpet the message that all the pseudo-Clausewitzes and self-appointed Palestinian beneficiaries of the "day after" dream seem to have on the tip of their tongue: "Look, we hear you; the peace process has been at a standstill for years. But we're getting it going again; and the Palestinian state that Israel didn't want, we're going to offer it to you forthwith." Delivering that message now would be a disgrace for at least two reasons.

First, the precondition for a state—today, like yesterday, and the day after, as well as the day before— is the existence of a dominant force among the

Palestinians that is prepared to say, "We are weary of war, and we accept the 1947 resolution that decreed the two states, despite the rejection of that resolution by our grandfathers, our fathers, and indeed, all of our leaders up to the present day." I have been waiting for that moment my entire adult life.

But are we there now? Have we heard anyone make this declaration?

Second, and most importantly, the business of the "day after" has an additional effect, one terrible not only for Israel, but for the entire world. Let us imagine that we say to the people of Gaza and the West Bank, "OK, we get it now. Before, our eyes didn't see, and our ears didn't hear; but this time, message received. Where the architects of peace failed, the terrorists, the Nazis, the pogromists have succeeded." Do people understand the implications of such a message? Do they have any idea of the victory that it would represent, not just for Hamas, but for every terrorist group on the planet? Would we not be traveling fifty years back in time, when terrorism was "the weapon of the poor," and therefore legitimate? Seeing crime pay off is the best way to encourage the criminal vocations that we feared would arise, like avenging jinnis, from the ruins of Mosul or Raqqa.

Justice for Palestinians who renounce terror and accept Israel, absolutely. A thousand times yes. But not like this. Not as a ransom extorted by the fear that jihadism kindles in us. Not, in other words, on the "day after."

8

Jacob, Solal, and Romain Gary

WE MUST CALL THINGS by their right name.

The truth is, the pogrom that should have been— and was, for a brief moment—the occasion for seamless solidarity with the dead and those who mourned them, produced the opposite effect: a gale of anti-Semitism. Or, to call it by its right name, a tempest of hatred for Jews without precedent since the Second World War.

East wind and west wind.

North wind and south wind.

The Latin America of my youth, when I supported opponents to dictatorship in Chile and Argentina, chanted in unison the dirge of the child-killing Jew.

The South Africa of Mandela, as if it were not enough to have hosted the Durban Conference with its awful slogan, "One Jew, One Bullet," seized the opportunity to level a charge of genocide against the Jewish state in the International Court of Justice, a crime originally defined to render justice to those murdered in the Holocaust.

The whole world, in fact, buzzed with the news, which seemed to warm the hearts of those whom the Jews had annoyed with their eternal pretension of being an exception to the law of massacres: "You too, Israelites, you who claimed not to kill, have killed; you too, so arrogant and sure of yourselves, victims transformed into executioners, are a domineering people. What if the Jewish people, after being, for decades, the exemplar of suffering, were to become the very emblem of crime, indiscriminate bombing, and extermination?"

The same was true, alas, in the two countries I know best, one because it is my native country; the other, the United States, because it is one of my emotional homelands.

In France, the number of anti-Semitic acts grew exponentially in the wake of October 7.

We saw rallies for the "Palestinian cause" at which participants were no longer afraid to shout, "Death to the Jews."

Universities became sites for the spray-painting of swastikas; wearing a yarmulke exposed one to insults or beating.

And the far left in the National Assembly, a faction that, in principle, is part of the democratic spectrum (where it has eclipsed the rest of the left) reconnected with the legacy of the doctrinally anti-Semitic wing of the workers' movement at the time of the Dreyfus Affair.

On the subject of Mr. Mélenchon and his ilk, I have one more observation to make.

We are too indulgent when we continue to give them credit for retaining a remnant of the spirit of French democratic republicanism.

We also give them too much credit if we see them as Machiavellians in search of a gimmick to help them pick up votes in low-income neighborhoods.

I keep a close eye on Mr. Mélenchon. I listen to what he says. I hear him when he refuses to "genuflect" before the council of French Jewish organizations, which no one ever asked him to do. Or when he accuses Élisabeth Borne, the then-prime minister, whose family history as survivors of the Holocaust he knows, of espousing "a foreign point of view." Or when he reproaches Yaël Braun-Pivet, president of the National Assembly, and a Jew who carries the same sort of wound in her heart, of "camping in Tel Aviv" and no longer speaking "in the name of the French people." Or criticizing Pierre Moscovici, president of the Court of Auditors, of not thinking "French," but rather "international finance."

Words have a history. And these words are cut-and-pasted from the rhetoric of the first Maurice Barrès, from Édouard Drumont of *La France juive*, and other anti-Semitic agitators of the Dreyfus Affair era. Just this morning, as I was about to sit down at my desk, I read a tweet from one of Mr. Mélenchon's flunkies with recommendations for Israeli athletes at the opening ceremony of the Paris Olympics. No flag, he says. No singing of the Olympic anthem. White uniform. All he forgot was the yellow star.

But the real shock came from the United States, whose founding fathers wanted the nation to become a new Jerusalem—and where, over a matter of days and among a part of the public, Jerusalem became the name of the worst of the worst.

We watched as demonstrations of support for "Palestine" filled Grand Central Terminal, blocked the Brooklyn Bridge, and vandalized libraries.

A strange slogan appeared in front of churches: "No Christmas as Usual!" It was clear enough that this referred, in the pure Marcionite tradition (I refer to the 12th-century Christian heresy named after Bishop Marcion, which sought to separate the Gospels from their Hebraic sources), to erasing Jesus's Jewish origins and magically transforming him into a crucified Palestinian Arab.

New York's uniformed police stood by with blank expressions as militants wearing keffiyehs and masks suggestive of the Ku Klux Klan flooded the streets calling for the eradication of Israel and published maps of Jewish organizations, foundations, and companies throughout the city that were designated "enemies of the Palestinian and colonized people" and therefore, presumably, fair game.

And there was, of course, the mudslide that occurred in some of the country's most prestigious universities.

Calls for hate and murder.

Harassment, intimidation, and physical aggression against Jewish students.

A Cornell professor, in a video with 12 million views, declared that the October 7 massacre had "exhilarated" him because it "shifted the balance of power."

Also at Cornell, a student was charged with threatening to "bring an assault rifle to campus and shoot all you pig Jews," to "stab" and "slit the throat" of Jewish men, to rape and "throw off a cliff" Jewish women, and to behead Jewish babies in imitation of Hamas.

Another individual suggested that the participants in the Nova music festival deserved what happened to them because they were partying "on stolen ground."

At Cooper Union in New York, terrified Jewish students were locked in the library for their own protection as a mob tried to bang down the doors.

At Pomona College in California, a shrine was erected to honor the "insurgents."

At Rutgers in New Jersey, an undergraduate was arrested for making death threats against Israeli students.

At Columbia and Barnard, on October 8, Professor Joseph Massad celebrated the attack as "awesome." On October 28, 144 faculty members signed a letter referring to the massacre of unarmed civilians as a "military action" and justified it as an "occupied people's right to resist."

Six months later, the campus was transformed into a hotbed of violence and hate at the "Gaza solidarity encampment" with chants of "We are Hamas," calls to become martyrs, and young people screaming that October 7 should be done "10,000 times." On the eve of Passover, a rabbi called for Jewish students to go home as their safety could no longer be guaranteed.

This cesspool of shame spread like wildfire, inspiring encampments at Yale, the University of North Carolina, the New School, to name a few...and I fear it is only beginning.

But the icing on the cake, the spectacle to end all spectacles, was the moment when the presidents of Harvard, MIT, and Penn appeared before the House

Committee on Education and the Workforce and clumsily skirted the issue. One after another, they were asked if these hateful words were constitutionally protected speech, or if calling for the destruction of Israel and the genocide of Jews constituted harassment and violated the regulations of their universities. Elizabeth Magill of MIT weakly replied that defining this sort of speech as harassment was a "context-dependent" decision.

When you realize that these three universities appear at the bottom of the free speech rankings compiled each year by the nonpartisan Foundation for Individual Rights and Expression, it is hard to avoid the following conclusion: All minorities on campus are protected against offensive comments; safe spaces and comfort zones are provided so students aren't inconvenienced by free but hurtful statements. That is, all minorities but one.

None of this is new, of course.

All of Israel's wars over the past half-century have given rise to similar eruptions of madness.

Moreover, the two are closely linked. In 1982, in one of my first books, I argued that blaming Jews has been a theme with many variations: first in the Christian era for killing Christ, then in the anti-Christian Enlightenment for having given birth to him, then in the socialist era for making common cause with capitalism, and then, with the advent of biology, for constituting a definitively foreign race—after all that, I showed how, in our own age, the words of hate most likely to reap the whirlwind are those that link the Jews to a previously demonized Israel. I posited that it is not so much that an anti-Zionist is necessarily anti-Semitic, but that there is no other way for a present-day anti-Semite to express his hate effectively than through the channel of hatred for Israel.

But this time around, the hate was immense.

It was as if the enormity of the crime against Israel made the rest of the sequence that much worse.

Or, as if one blamed oneself for feeling the shock that the shock had produced and needed to be forgiven for the moment of distraction and vacillation during which the world communed, for an instant, with the attacked Israelis, before being overtaken by a blunt, mad, and almost limitless hatred.

So, baby-killing Jews.

Jews who, as in the time of Shylock or Pharaoh, cut their pound of flesh from the living body of the world.

Jews guilty of murdering the modern Christ, that is, the Palestinians of Gaza.

Jews guilty of causing famine, poisoning wells, drinking the blood of their victims.

Jews guilty of being Jews, upon whom one attempts to hang a yellow star, not on their clothes but on their hearts.

Jews guilty, through one last twist of irrationality in the mad woke vision of the world, not of being a "race," but of *not* being one. It seems they have become the white man's surrogates, one with the detested West that for a thousand years sought their destruction.

And this wall of incomprehension (one might say a pyramid) upon which words break when one tries to explain that Israel is a small country fighting, not to expand, not to replace, not to oppress, not to exterminate, but to survive, and to prevent those who tore away the lives of 1,200 of its children in a display of savagery that shocked the world from repeating that barbarous act.

It was, it is, a tidal wave of hate.

Israel does have friends, of course.

There is President Biden, who has affirmed Israel's right to self-defense. But alas, the president has constructed a set of red lines that are not necessarily compatible with Israel's security and victory. Will he hold his own against the ascendant radicals in his party? This is becoming less and less clear as the months pass and the US election approaches. And although the United States stood by Israel when Iran attacked it on April 13 with an unprecedented barrage of missiles and drones, what are we to make of the calls for Israeli "restraint"? Of the exhortations for Israel to "take the win" and stand down in the face of this aggression? How should we take this warning, repeated in every register: "If Israel is tempted to respond to Iran; if it feels the need to prevent a repetition, as in Gaza; if it decides to strike Iran's nuclear facilities, which everyone knows would be a hair's breadth from the final threshold, well, then, it will do so without its American ally"?

There are Republicans and Democrats, people across the political spectrum, who understand that, far from being an apartheid state, Israel is one of the most successful multiethnic democracies in the world, as well as a key American ally. But will they be heard?

There are Christians of integrity who understand the part of themselves that the Jewish people embody and how, without their existential obstinacy, their determination to remain rooted in their origin, which is also their destination, Christianity itself would be in danger. But this is the eternal question: These sisters and brothers in our shared Judeo-Christian heritage—how many divisions do they have?

Israel has friends in the Arab-Muslim world who have understood—for example, in Kurdistan—that this war is their war as well. But here too, what weight do they carry? And what price will they have to pay for such brave honesty?

Israel had, in my country, old friends on the liberal side of the political spectrum. But how can we count on the French socialists or ecologists when they form a fraudulent electoral union with Mélenchon, even with the worthy goal of stopping the extreme right from gaining control of France's National Assembly following Macron's dissolution in the wake of the European parliamentary elections? Do they not see and smell the rancid anti-Semitism with which they are aligning themselves?

Finally, there are the new friends of Israel occupying the far-right corners of Western political chessboards, many of whom seem to have extended a supportive hand. But what are we to make of them? Can they be counted on? I pose the question sincerely. I am not forgetting that people can and do change, that parties can be transformed, or that examples can be found of recovering racists, repentant anti-Semites, and children of fascists breaking with the heritage of their fathers.

But is that the case here?

In France, can Marine Le Pen honestly claim to have broken with the views of her famously anti-Semitic father, Jean-Marie Le Pen, when she treats wearing a kippa and wearing an Islamist veil with equal opprobrium? Or when she continues (the last we heard) to reject Jacques Chirac's bold words acknowledging France's responsibility in the 1942 deportation of Jews and the culpability of the Vichy regime in the Holocaust?

And what of Jordan Bardella, president of the extreme right party, Rassemblement National, who seems incapable of answering the question of whether Jean-Marie Le Pen was or was not anti-Semitic when he mused about the "batch" that should be made of the descendants of Holocaust survivors who had the temerity to stand up to him, or when he opined that the gas chambers were a mere "detail" in the history of the Second World War? Can Mr. Bardella really affirm without blinking that he has made the long, difficult, painful, and necessary journey to extricate oneself from the prejudices of anti-Semitism?

What are we to make of the former collaborators of Le Pen who were pushed aside due to their openly fascist inclinations but who prowl like jackals around the edges of the party?

And how should we view, in the United States, the evangelical Christians who are a mainstay of Donald Trump's support? Yes, they are nominally "Zionists." But only to the extent that they expect on Judgment Day to take Israel's place on the very land where the Jewish state presently and provisionally stands. Are these really Israel's friends? Isn't theirs a path opposite that of the Christians of integrity who consider the Jews, not mere guardians of the holy sites who will be, at the end of time, converted or destroyed, but as brothers in faith?

And what of Donald Trump himself, who, when asked about his personal relationship with the Jews, responded that "short guys wearing yarmulkes" are the only people he wants counting his money?

Then there is Viktor Orbán, whom I first met as a young dissident when the Berlin Wall came down and reencountered thirty years later in Budapest, in his new garb as prime minister, expressing to me—in the same sentence—his solidarity with Israel and his admiration for Miklós Horthy, the Hungarian Pétain and one of those chiefly responsible for the deportation of 437,000 Hungarian Jews to Auschwitz in 1944?

No.

That is not how people change.

One does not break with anti-Semitism by decree, with the stroke of a pen.

And while I am well aware that a nation as fragile as Israel cannot afford the luxury of refusing a helping hand, in this case, I recommend extreme caution.

I still remember the philosopher Pierre Boutang, a genuinely repentant anti-Semite, explaining to me the far right's divine surprise when it learned that the people previously lost, exiled, and wandering stood again among the ranks of modern nations.

I remember discovering passages, around the time I was writing *L'Idéologie Française* (1981), in which Édouard Drumont, the Jew-hating journalist and politician who founded the Antisemitic League of France in 1889, applauded the birth of Zionism, which he saw as a return to the fold of the recalcitrant black sheep.

For men like these to admit in good faith that they recognize any greatness in Israel apart from its return to the fold of normal nations and any utility of the Jews other than blocking the return of the

Saracens—this should be a precondition for participating in an informed discussion of this question.

And the Jews, every Jew, likewise in good conscience, must ponder the worth of any alliance that is not based on true friendship, sincere respect, or some knowledge, however vague, of the adventure of Judaism, of Jewish memory, and what it means to be a Jew. That too should be a minimum requirement, given that Jews have paid so dearly for their past blindness to the machinery of evil.

Speaking strictly for myself, things seem clear.

No alliance can be worth a renunciation by the Jews of the duty of exceptionalism, which from Akiva to Kafka and from Rashi to Proust, has been the yeast of their almost incomprehensible resistance.

Nothing excuses our forgetting that the endurance of the Jewish people through the ages was also fed by their rejection of anything resembling contempt for the stranger, hate for the other, racism, or chauvinism, all of which are forms of idolatry.

And assuming that these things are not forgotten, care must still be taken not to mingle even a drop of the ink of divine light with which the books of Jewish wisdom were written with the bile and venom that these new friends heap on other vulnerable peoples. No accord is possible, no historic compromise is conceivable, with "friends" such as these.

The Jews, therefore, are alone.

Decidedly, dramatically alone.

And their solitude is all the more tragic because the small but great nation of Israel, this thin strip of land attacked on all sides and jeered at by billions of people who have forgotten what they owe it, this people constantly found guilty and at fault, constantly stigmatized, is caught between two fires, tossed about like a doll, pulled between liberal forces that resemble it but disavow it and illiberal forces that do not resemble it, but defend it.

However.

Tragedy is Greek, not Jewish.

The major task of a Jew is not, like Oedipus at Colonus, to determine that the gods are cruel and that irreconcilable forces run the world behind our backs; it is to survive.

And from this point of view, yes, the Jews are more alone than they have ever been.

Or perhaps a variation on this theme would be more accurate.

Perhaps they are alone, as it was always said they would be, just more desperately so.

I think of Jacob who, after slaving away for so long, reaches Abraham's promised land and finds himself surrounded by a pack of dogs—and sits.

I think of the writer Albert Cohen repeating to me the lesson of Solal from his masterpiece, *Belle du Seigneur*, at our meetings on the Avenue Krieg in Geneva; urging me to excel, to steel myself, to play the Greek before the Gentiles, to practice their rituals; and then warning me, suddenly anxious, sounding like a man awakened in the middle of a nightmare, that even if I did so, it would last only for a while because, from time immemorial, the Beast always wins in the end.

I think of the writer Romain Gary, the other friend whom I believed, as many did, to be on the side of Jewish strength. I can still see him, haughty, playing proud, his bony cheeks of burnished steel under the Astrakan cap that he wore throughout our lunch. I can still hear him, speaking too loudly in the fine voice of a mountain man who has triumphed over war and death, sound and silence, blame and glory, urging me on to ruse and resist, with humor and love. "Death to the bastards," he shouted that day to me and everyone else in the restaurant. "We'll get them! You'll get them! They won't be able to resist the Dybbuk that a seasoned Jew like you will shove up their ass! Don't be scared!" And then, lower, from the gut, pale under the red of his cheeks: "But for how long? In fact, it's all over; we're taking up too much room. Our existence is outrageous. I've known from the beginning that we're expendable." A few weeks later, he was dead.

And then I think one last time of Emmanuel Levinas's haunting words in *Proper Names*, already quoted above.

But in my thinking today, it is not only our mansions of the Boulevard Haussmann that are being looted and burned, but our apartments large and small; our fancy and not-so-fancy neighborhoods; the synagogues humble and soaring. It is our Shabbats, when we observe them, our small holidays and grand bar mitzvahs, our Hannukah menorahs and tiny candlesticks, the Sukkot set up after Yom Kippur, which to me suggest straw creatures apt to go up in smoke or fly away. For those not observant, it is a night that begins when there are no longer humble Jews or great Jews, studious Jews or secular Jews; where there are no longer Jewish politicians, journalists, artists, philosophers, shopkeepers, businessmen, doctors, lawyers, or judges. Only Jews. Culprits.

PART THREE

History and Truth

9

Why Israel

WHY ISRAEL?

This is the first question posed by those inflamed by the topic. It seems simple. But it's actually very complicated.

Claude Lanzmann, in his very first film, shot in 1972 in the aftermath of the Six Day War, and before his famous epic, *Shoah*, asked this same question and entitled his work: *Why Israel.*

No question mark—just a simple assertion, made with his massive authority.

But it was still a question.

Why a state rather than nothing? Why a state instead of assimilation, the end of Jewish exceptionalism, and peace for households and nations? Why a state instead of resolving the contradictions, finding a new formula, forming a grand alliance? For so long, Christianity, Hegelianism, socialism, and the whole world have been appealing to the Jews: "We gave you everything, granted you so much; we took on your Genesis, we went along with your one God and renounced our national gods for him. Now that that's done, calm down, be nice, be realistic, broad-minded, accommodating; join up with the hearts and minds of the rest of us in the building of humanity. Don't you see that your position is untenable, that you're sailing into the wind? Don't you realize that your nation will be a ghetto, a shtetl, an open-air prison, a zone of exclusion, and if things take a bad turn, a quarantine zone? You should have woken up a century ago, at the time of the awakening of nations, instead of waiting until now!"

Or to put it in a kinder form: Why a mere state rather than everything? Why a state rather than the painful but glorious destiny of life in the diaspora, a life rich in incomparable human adventures and profound spiritual accomplishments? Why a state rather than universality, humanization of the other, and the vital cosmopolitanism that for so long were the vocation of the Jews? The Judaism of the human Torah…the practice of the Talmud and its invisible temples…faith in a God believed not to have come only for the Jews, but also for those not here with them today…. Was there not a better destiny for all of that, frankly, than to find oneself pinned to a strip of land that represents, as your Book says, a tiny fraction of humanity?

The question is not trivial.

More than a few great figures of Judaism have posed it conscientiously.

It is the topic of a polemic in the early 1920s between Gershom Scholem, the German-Israeli philosopher who planned to return to the Jewish homeland as soon as it emerged from limbo, and Franz Rosenzweig, author of *The Star of Redemption* and the inspiration for Levinas, who chose to remain in Frankfurt rather than emigrate. Scholem had no illusions about the future of Judaism in Germany and found hope only in a renaissance of the Jewish people in their own land. Rosenzweig, who was no less concerned about the continuity of Jewish life, expressed doubt about a return to Zion, which he saw as a path toward the normalization of Judaism, and refused to part ways with the uniqueness and the strangeness associated with life in the diaspora.

On December 26, 1926, three years after a dispute that Scholem later described (in *From Berlin to Jerusalem*) as the stormiest of his life, and while he was giving shape to his dream and living in Jewish Palestine, he sent his friend an oddly melancholic letter in which he decried the ravages "done to the Hebraic language by its passage from the status of a sacred language to one of commerce and communication" and from which he concluded (as if admitting that Rosenzweig had been right) that "this profaning of the language" is the sign of a "process of normalization" that "imperils the very essence of tradition."

This was the thinking of Rosenzweig and Scholem. Also of Levinas, who like Rosenzweig made it a point of honor not to drop the Greek substance for its Hebrew shadow. It was the thinking of Judah Leon Magnes, one of the most prominent voices of American Reform Judaism, the great organizer of the New York Jewish community, and the first chancellor of the Hebrew University of Jerusalem, who died the year of Israel's founding and never disavowed the fragile but precious benefits of an exile conceived as an antidote to the Canaanite Judaism that he saw taking root in Tel Aviv.

Such was the thinking, too, of many Jews of the generation of Claude Lanzmann and myself. Not the French and German Israelites of the 1930s who, like Léon Brunschvicg, Marc Bloch, or Hermann Cohen, believed that the highest contribution of Judaism was to have invented, through the Law, human rights. But rather, Sartrean Jews. Jews not concerned or ashamed about being Jews. Jewish figures of my youth who, like Benny Lévy and Pierre Goldman, were proudly putting what remained of their Judaism in the service of revolution. Didn't they see their role as extending a hand to those in distress, to the poor, and to souls deemed lost, just as Jonah had done? And that the

"chosen people" were the *Am Segulah*, the secret trea-
sure needed by nations that wish to renounce their part
in inhumanity and join others on the path of redemption? And I wrote later, in *The Genius of Judaism*, that
the task of the Jews is to repair the world.

So yes, it is a real question.

To this real question, Lanzmann responded in
word and deed that Israel is certainly the historical
homeland of the Jewish people.

He knew that the return to Zion, with the books
of the Bible as his guide, as they had been for the first
Zionists, was a good and just thing.

He also thought, I surmise, that if the Jewish
exception was to endure for the benefit of the nations
of the world, as well as for the Jews, it was of capital
importance that the Jewish exception have a capital, a
physical place where Jewish thought could be quick-
ened and put into practice.

But the heart of his response hinged on one word.
Just one. A terrible and bloody word. A word that
made even the most unreligious of us shudder. A word
that shook even the atheists who thought, as Freud
put it in a letter to the German Jewish writer Arnold
Zweig, that "the national idea poisons the nerves and
the blood." A word that induced second thoughts
in modern unbelievers like Lanzmann and me, who
prefer people to rocks and have never really understood how one can organize one's life around stories

of old walls, tombs, sacred stones, and empty temples. That word is anti-Semitism.

Yes, indeed.

The old hatred.

The oldest of all hatreds.

The one that pursued the Jews from Babylon to Persia.

From Persia to a Judea first invaded and then deserted by the Romans who, before leaving, sacked Jerusalem and, according to Flavius Josephus, filled its trickling streams with the blood of thousands of Jews.

The hate that, when Rome became Christian and Jews had to flee to the Rhineland, Provence, or Spain to escape the mobs that hounded them, destroyed the Jewish communities, where science, intellectual beauty, and moral intensity were as bright as new.

The hatred in ultra-Christian France, where from Philip Augustus to Saint Louis, from Philip the Handsome to Louis the Quarrelsome and Charles VI, sovereigns never ceased extorting money from Jews, expelling them, and then inviting them back to be extorted anew. The hatred that took Jews hostage and exchanged them, not for assassins as in Gaza, but for the money they had lent to the kingdom which the kingdom now wanted them to relinquish; the hatred of a France that witnessed, in Rashi of Troyes, the dawning of the most beautiful of Talmudic suns, but then used the everlasting Jewish sin—rejection of the

Cross—to justify persecuting his descendants. You say Roman legions scourged the body of Rabbi Akiva with iron rakes? Scalped Rabbi Ishmael while he wore his tefillin? Pulled out the tongue of the interpreter of the last yeshiva left standing after the Bar Kokhba revolt? It was in Ramerupt, in the Champagne region of France, that the bloody corpse of Rabbeinu Tam, Rashi's grandson, was tied to a horse's tail and dragged over the stones of the village streets.

I am referring to the hatred that, when the Jews left France and their friend Pascal could not find them because they had all disappeared, pursued them farther east, farther and farther east: to Poland, Lithuania, Ukraine, Transylvania; to Prague where, as Kafka wrote, people "bathe in hatred of the Jew"; all the way to the tundras and taigas of Russia. Everywhere were pogroms, relentless pogroms; an endless loop of massacres and raids. Inspiring the most harrowing novels of Isaac Bashevis Singer, there were the stories of Nathan Hannover who, in 1648, saw women whose bellies were slit so that live cats could be sewn in; children skewered with lances and hacked into pieces to be hawked in the street like meat or roasted on spits and brought back to their mothers, who were forced to eat them.

It is the same hate that during the Dreyfus Affair made half of a great country rise up to defend a modest Jewish captain who had been unjustly sentenced, while the other half clamored for his death just because he was Jewish.

And then the epitome of that hatred, its height, the unprecedented modern event of no return, the technical and industrialized anti-Judaism that reached its climax in the darkest days of the Holocaust.

The post-Holocaust world thought it could contain that event in an intellectual sarcophagus as tight as Chernobyl—but it was a Maginot Line.

There you are.

Lanzmann is not the oft-victorious Jewish Orpheus crossing the Acheron to find his Eurydice of six million faces that the Nazis had wanted to turn into a mist.

But he knows all that.

He knows that there are happy Jews and unhappy Jews, obscure Jews and luminous Jews, cursed Jews and exultant Jews, transgressive Jews, self-hating Jews, and naive Jews who believe, each time and to the end, that empires, kingdoms, and republics will protect their rights. But he also knows that one thing they all have in common is the constant possibility of falling prey to the Beast and its unlimited voracity.

For all of them, he says, Israel provides a recourse.

For all, if the horde catches up with them, Israel offers a refuge.

For all, he insists, the hatred that pursues the Jews and nearly swallowed them was a necessary and sufficient reason for Israel's birth.

And for all those haunted, in 2024 as in 1945, by Adorno's oath to do everything he could, absolutely everything, to ensure that "Auschwitz is not repeated," Israel is self-evident.

It is as simple as that.

It was time for the nations of the world to give a breath of air to what remained of the Jewish people after making it breathe in the smell of its incinerated men, women, and children.

A millionth of the planet, if they wanted it, for the survivors of the people that gave the Book to humanity and is the oldest of its persecuted peoples.

That is what the state's declaration of independence says in fitting terms: "The Nazi holocaust" demonstrates "the urgency of solving the problem of [Jewish] homelessness by re-establishing in Eretz-Israel the Jewish State."

Why Israel?

That's why.

10

Colonialism?

THE SECOND QUESTION is that of colonialism.

Not the colonies in the West Bank. Not the settlements created since 1967 by successive governments of Israel in that part of the land set aside for a new Arab state after the second World War—settlements that Israel will have to dismantle one day.

No. Those who use this term mean something else. They mean that Israel itself is a "colonial phenomenon."

And they think that Israel in its entirety is a "Western colony."

That, too, provoked great anger in Claude Lanzmann. Even more so because the debate on this question in France had been launched in a notorious special issue of *Les Temps modernes*, Jean-Paul Sartre's magazine, which appeared shortly before the Six-Day

War. The entire issue was devoted to the Israeli⬜Palestinian conflict and contained an article by the Marxist scholar, Maxime Rodinson, entitled "Israel, Colonial Phenomenon."

"Can you believe it?" Lanzmann said to me, his beautiful dark voice full of contentiousness.

"The Exodus, a colonial phenomenon?

"The songs of the ghetto, a colonial phenomenon?

"The Spartacist songs of Gert Granach that I used in the opening credits of *Shoah*, the kibbutz of Gan-Shmuel and its cedar groves, Shmuel Bogler, the Auschwitz survivor, Simha Flapan, the father of the new historians and of far-left Zionism, all of the characters and figures of my film—a 'colonial phenomenon'?"

I listened as he recited, in a tone of outworn patience, entire passages from the article by Rodinson, his former friend, passages he still knew by heart: "I believe that I have demonstrated by the foregoing that the formation of the state of Israel on Palestinian land is the culmination of a process that fits squarely within the larger movement of European-American expansion during the 19th and 20th centuries to populate or dominate other lands."

Lanzmann was right, of course. And now, fifty years later, it is astonishing to see this old refrain return amid the chaos and confusion unleashed by the new war.

So let's make it very clear.

Israel is not a colonial artifact for the plain and simple reason that there have always been Jews on the land that is the state of Israel today. Always. Even during the time of the Romans and their brutal ethnic cleansing, indigenous Jews were living in the hills and deserts, descendants of the contemporaries of the Second Temple who had never budged. And the others, all the others forced onto the roads of exile, never passed a day without reciting the nostalgic and vehement Psalm 126, never knowing whether it should be spoken in the past or future tense, but that was—this much is certain—the setting of Jewish history, Jewish suffering, and Jewish hope for two millennia:

> When the Lord restored the fortunes of Zion, we were like those who dreamed. Our mouths were filled with laughter, our tongues with songs of joy. Then it was said among the nations, 'The Lord has done great things for them.' Restore our fortunes, Lord, like streams in the Negev. Those that sow in tears shall reap with songs of joy.

Captives are not colonists. Sowing with tears and harvesting joy is the language of dreams, not of subservience, appropriation, and conquest.

The second reason why Israel is not and cannot be a colonial artifact is that, although those indigenous Jews were obviously not organized into a nation in the sense of the term today, neither were the indigenous Arabs. This is a subject that preoccupied the early Zionists, as attested by an anecdote reported by Martin Buber in which the Zionist physician and writer Max Nordau runs to Theodor Herzl's home, frantic: I've just learned, he says in substance, that there are Arabs in Palestine; aren't we about to harm another nation? The reality, as Herzl knew, is that this people, who had been known as Palestinian since the Romans gave them that name (thinking back to the Philistines), had been living there for ages, but in no way thought of themselves as making up a nation. And the Palestinian representatives at the first congress of Muslim and Christian organizations in Jerusalem ten years earlier spoke explicitly to this point: We are, they said, "an integral part of Arab Syria, from which we have never been separated."

To which the enemies of Israel object: "Fine. But the number? The proportion? Weren't the Palestinians—whether they sprang from the Phoenicians, the Philistines, or another people, and whether or not they thought of themselves as part of Arab Syria—far more numerous than the Jews?" That is true. And no one contests it. But one must also consider the state of things in 1947, the year of the United Nations resolution creating two states on the territory of Mandatory Palestine. At that time, the indigenous Jews made up a third of the population in the territory that was to be divided. And in the portion that they were to receive, the Jews made up about half.

This point is critical. When the dispute about the two nations began, there were as many Jews as Arabs, as many indigenous Jews as indigenous Arabs, on the land that we're now told "a colonial state" was formed. And while it is true that Jewish migration sped up in the 1930s, that was not because Europe was sending Jews as the vanguard of some colonial project, but because the Nazis were in the process of annihilating them.

"You're acting as if there is only one kind of colonialism," comes the reply, "the French kind, for example, with its expeditionary forces, its artillery, and its gunboats seizing Algeria. Aren't there other forms of colonization, slower and subtler, by which another people's land is stolen little by little?" No doubt. But in the muddle of historians' debates over the Israeli–Palestinian conflict, there is one point on which all agree. Colonization is theft. But in this case, there was neither theft nor fraud. The lands acquired by the migrants and the indigenous Jews alike were not stolen but legally purchased. Indeed, under the reign of the Ottomans, and after 1920, the British, those lands were the subject of fervent speculation. It was not unusual to see a parcel purchased for a given amount and then flipped for ten or twenty times that much. And while it is true that the new owners had an ideology that required them to work the land themselves and thus displaced the tenant farmers or day laborers who had been working it up to that point, it is not true that the lands of the future state of Israel were taken from their rightful owners by force or fraud or in defiance of the law.

In that case, what about the war that followed Israel's declaration of independence? Was that not the occasion for the massive expulsion that the Palestinians call the "Nakba," where they suffered a Holocaust of some sort, as documented by Tom Segev, Avi Shlaim, Benny Morris, and the other so-called "new historians"? Here too, however, one must be precise. One must not forget that the war began with an invasion by five Arab armies in May 1948, immediately after the British withdrawal. Nor can one forget that this was preceded by appeals from Arab religious and political leaders to "fight for every inch of their country" (from the chairman of the Arab High Commission), to shed "the last drop of their blood for their land" (from the spokesman of the Arab High Commissioner to the UN), and to carry out "a war of extermination," an "immense massacre" that will be talked about "as much as the massacres of Mongolia and the Crusades" (Azzam Pasha, Secretary-General of the Arab League). But, above all, one must be precise.

That there were expulsions is certain: Benny Morris, the historian who examined this issue with the greatest care, estimates that some 15 percent of the departures were forced. That the Jewish armed forces also committed acts of violence to sow terror is also true:

an example is Deir Yassin, where 100 to 120 villagers were killed during a pitched battle between foreign Arab fighters and Jewish militias on April 9, 1948. But most of the 700,000 departures for Lebanon, Jordan, or Egypt fell into two groups, as acknowledged even by the researchers most keen to contest the Zionists' account. In the first group were distressed civilians, who decided, as in any war, to leave the combat zones in the path of the invading Arab armies to seek safety. The second, unique to this war, was made up of those who heeded calls to leave by leaders of local tribes, neighboring states, and the "High Command of Arab Volunteers for the Liberation of Palestine," who promised a prompt return in Arab army trucks once the nascent Jewish state had been destroyed. No one should minimize the suffering of families uprooted from the land where their forebears were born. Just as no one should ignore the fate of that other set of refugees: the 700,000 Jews who, at the same time, were given twenty-four hours to leave the neighboring Arab states with nothing but the clothes on their backs. But words have a meaning. And here, the words do not support the thesis of colonialization.

There is one last reason why the colonial lexicon is not applicable to the birth of Israel. References to colonialism are also references to its source. Now, the reality is that the source in this case, which was Great

Britain, opposed strenuously, here as elsewhere, the disruption of its empire.

Of course, the 1917 Balfour Declaration had been greeted with an explosion of joy in Jewish communities worldwide. Signed by Foreign Secretary Arthur Balfour, formerly prime minister and first lord of the admiralty, it began with these astonishing words: "His Majesty's Government view with favour the establishment in Palestine of a national home for the Jewish people, and will use their best endeavours to facilitate the achievement of this object." But this declaration was followed six weeks later by another, signed by General Allenby, victor at the battles of Gaza (November 1917) and Jerusalem (December 1917) to the effect that: "Palestine will be neither Jewish nor Arab; it will be English."

It is easy to forget the political context of the event—that is, a moment when the British Empire was looking for every possible alliance, Jewish or Arab, Arab or Jewish, to defeat its Ottoman rival. It is even easier to forget that, in the period that immediately followed the fall of the Ottomans, and again in 1945 with the capitulation of Nazi Germany, it was Soviet bloc governments and liberal Americans who were advocating the establishment of a Jewish state, while His Majesty's government was doing everything it could to slow Jewish immigration; everything to block, where it could, the purchase of land; everything, in short, to put out the fire that Balfour had started.

I recommend reading Joseph Kessel's reports in *France-Soir* at the end of Israel's war of independence. They reveal a colonial power that was doing the Jews no favors.

One reads about Haganah and Irgun waging a fierce guerilla war against the British.

And one discovers that the Mandate, when the time came to retreat, preferred to leave their bases to the Arab Legion, which was, by the way, commanded until the very last day by an English officer.

Israel's independence thus falls within a double context.

One is the growth of nationalism, a movement into which its entry was late and staggered.

The second is the history of empires, but in the direction opposite the one usually invoked: Israel is the fruit of a war of emancipation, not the establishment of a colony. Its birth is a moment in the history not of empires but of their dissolution; and Zionism itself is not a form of imperialism but of anti-imperialism.

That is the reality of Zionism, despite its status as the new international curse word.

That is Zionism seen plainly, and not disguised in the ideological garb of its denigrators.

Zionism, in short, like every other Jewish adventure, did not arise in order to gain power and dominate the world. It emerged as a new solution for the survival of a people who encountered no more and no less incomprehension, hostility, and destructive will on this path than they had endured along the routes of the diaspora.

11

Radical Islam

FINE, OBJECT THE TIRELESS anti-Zionists. Let's admit that Israel's independence was won through sheer determination and against the will of empires rather than an extension of their policies of dispossession and displacement.

The fact remains that it was blessed by other nations because they saw it as a way of making up for the crime of the Holocaust.

The question then becomes, Why here? Why on this ground? Why make an Arab nation pay for a crime committed by Germans? Couldn't Israel have been created in Bavaria, or Schleswig-Holstein?

Merely to ask such a question ignores the ancient presence of the Jews on this land, which I have already discussed. But it has a pseudo-obviousness that appeals to young minds concerned with equity and justice, so I feel the need to properly respond to it.

First, there is the metaphysical response: Was the Holocaust a crime against humanity or not? If so, the very nature of such a crime is that it affects man as a "species" (per Robert Antelme, a survivor of Buchenwald); it casts his very being into doubt (see Primo Levi's *If This Is a Man*); it provokes an "eclipse" of the human (in the words of Hannah Arendt). There is a *metaphysical* culpability, as Karl Jaspers argued in *The Question of German Guilt*, that is distinct from the *personal* culpability of the individuals who committed the crime, the *political* culpability of the state that gave the orders, and the *moral* culpability that is a matter of conscience for each of us. Metaphysical culpability implicates humanity as a whole; no human anywhere can escape it.

But there is also a response that is purely historical and concrete: Although the Nazi project was indeed conceived in Europe, and although it was Germany, a European country, that mobilized all of its forces to achieve the supreme goal of exterminating the Jews, the execution of the crime did not come down to Germany alone. It involved other actors on all continents; and the Arab world, or the Arab-Muslim world, was less innocent in this regard than it lets on.

Here enters another group of new historians, one that does not constitute a school but whose members in Germany (Matthias Küntzel), the United States (Jeffrey Herf), and the United Kingdom (David Motadel) have documented the connections between Nazism and the Arab-Muslim world. These scholars have established three facts.

1. The existence, well before the war, of an Arab form of Nazism, exemplified by the birth of the Muslim Brotherhood. "Is Nazism not a great ideological invention of our time?" asked Hassan al-Banna, co-founder of the Brotherhood. "Is it not a vigorous response to the crisis of the liberal model whose decadence we see everywhere around us? And why should the Arab nation deprive itself of the benefits it stands to gain from a regional version of the Nazi model?" It was in that spirit that al-Banna founded the Brotherhood. He was thinking of Nazism when, in a 1938 editorial, he lauded the ideal of an Arab "industry of death." That is also what the Egyptian street was thinking when the Muslim Brotherhood (then with 200,000 members) distributed Arabic translations of *Mein Kampf* and the *Protocols of the Elders of Zion* as brown-shirted students staged violent demonstrations shouting, "Down with Jews!" and "Jews out of Egypt and Palestine!"

2. Once the war began, the rallying of a large part of the Arab world to the Axis powers in general and to Germany in particular. Not the entire Arab world, of course. Not Morocco, for example, whose heroic

sultan declared his support for the Allies and, when the Vichy government asked him to require Morocco's 200,000 Jews to wear the yellow star, responded: "There are no Jews living in the Protectorate, there are only Moroccan subjects." If Vichy insisted, he continued, please "provide 50 additional stars for members of the royal family." Nor did it apply to the tens of thousands of Arabs and Berbers who fought in Free France units. (In May 1944, my own father, along with Moroccan *tabor* and *goumier* light infantry units, scaled the last peaks of the highest summit of Monte Cassino.) Nor to the thousands of Palestinians who fought side by side with Jewish comrades in the Palestine Infantry Companies formed by the British army in 1940 to fight in Syria, Egypt, and Cyrenaica.

But rallying to the Axis is indeed the right term for Antoun Saadeh, founder of a Syrian national socialist party that is today linked to Hezbollah. Likewise for Zaki al-Arsuzi, another admirer of the Nazi regime and the inspiration for the two branches of the Ba'athist party, one in Iraq and the other in Syria until the advent of Bashar al-Assad. There was Libya as well, since it was, like Somalia and Eritrea, under Italian dominion, along with the Young Egypt party, whose leaders were invited to Nazi party congresses and even participated in Wehrmacht maneuvers.

There is also the case of Rashid Ali al-Gaylani, prime minister of the Kingdom of Iraq, who engaged in armed confrontation with the British. Defeated in May 1941 at Basra, he fled to Berlin, where Hitler recognized him as head of the Iraqi government in exile. Baghdad was also a center of the Al-Futuwwa fascist youth movement. Its Palestinian incarnation, formed at the same time, in the same spirit, and with the same ideals, saturated the radio waves with calls for a regeneration of Arab youth in the mold of the Hitlerjugend. Many similar youth movements emerged from a strange cultural stew in which were mingled an anti-Westernism claiming its philosophical roots in Heidegger and a cult of the superman drawn from the half-baked Nietzschian idea that Hitler was the "great adventurer" capable of straddling history, shaping it, and in the process ridding the world of Anglo-American imperialism. German radio propaganda in Egypt presented the Führer as another Mohammed and Germany's Volksgemeinschaft, its national community forged in iron and blood, as an analogue to the Muslim Ummah.

3. Then we have Amin al-Husseini, the much-discussed Grand Mufti of Jerusalem. He is better known. Less well known is the fact that the British appointed him to his position shortly after the pogroms of 1920, which he personally had a hand in organizing.

Can we fathom the disappointment of the Jews, who had been dazzled, like moths around a flame, by the Balfour Declaration and were now being burned by its swift retraction?

Can we grasp the radicalism of the conversion of this man with the dreaming face, a face that was probably not altered by the race-related ravings of the Nazis he befriended?

Or his move in 1941 to Zeesen, south of Berlin, where he broadcasted fanatical anti-Jewish diatribes throughout the Middle East?

Or his possible influence on Himmler, whom he seems to have dissuaded from exchanging, in 1943, 20,000 German prisoners for 5,000 Jewish children seeking emigration to Palestine?

Or his contact with Hitler, whom he later claimed to have advised, and their November 1941 meeting, where he expresses his solidarity in view of the fact that they had the "same enemies, namely the English, the Jews and the Communists."

Or the confirmation of that advisory role by Dieter Wisliceny, Adolf Eichmann's deputy, who declared at the Nuremberg trial that "the Grand Mufti, who lived in Berlin after 1941, played a role of non-negligible importance in the German government's decision to exterminate Europe's Jews."

Or his fairly accurate knowledge of what the Reich meant by "final solution," when he declared in November 1943 that Germany "has been able to expose the Jews and has decided to find a definitive solution to the Jewish danger."

Or his comparison, in Frankfurt of that same year, of the Jews to "disease-carrying insects."

Or his recruitment of an SS unit posted in Athens that, if Rommel were victorious in Egypt, would pounce on Palestine and liquidate the embryonic Jewish state. That this unit never had a chance to fulfill its evil purpose does not mitigate the Mufti's intention.

The fact that Arab commentators (including Palestinians) ignore this dark page of their history; that this part of the world should be the only one never to have acknowledged, documented, and taught its participation in the supreme crime of the Holocaust; and that PLO leader Yasser Arafat should have continued to the end to embrace the Mufti—all of this speaks volumes about the appeal and ongoing vitality of this unspoken Nazism.

In short, Arab Nazism was a fact, and this region, too, experienced the battle between Nazism and anti-Nazism.

Global crime, in other words, is not an empty phrase, nor is "crime against humanity" a formula for use only by lawyers and moralists.

The foregoing account succinctly negates the myth of an innocent Palestine, uninvolved in Hitler's war against the Jews, that has been made to bear the burden of reparations for the crime of the Holocaust.

12

His Brother's Keeper?

Now comes the most difficult question.

It is not a historical question but an open one.

It is the question of civilian deaths in Gaza, including the death of children.

I won't attempt to skirt the issue.

Nor will I say there "are no words" for such an abomination. Or that, in the face of the outrageous death of civilians, particularly children, words wilt, die, and tumble into the chasm of what cannot be said.

Nor will I enter into the dispute over numbers, particularly as those figures, coming from the Hamas Ministry of Health, are necessarily dubious and do not separate out combatants disguised as civilians and civilians hit as if they were combatants.

For a dead person is a dead person.

A civilian death is a civilian death.

And among the many outrages posed by these deaths, there is none greater, for myself and anyone else who has been a father or mother, or who dreams of becoming one, than the death of a child who could have been one's own. The death of children is the ultimate outrage, as it has been since there has been a world. From Athens to Jerusalem to the India of Prince Siddhārtha Gautama, it is the absolute metaphysical scandal.

I said it in Bosnia.

I said it in Darfur and Angola.

I said it exactly fifty years ago in Ma'a lot-Tarshiha, in the north of Israel, where twenty-two school children who had been taken hostage were executed with a grenade by a terrorist group that was not Hamas.

I said it again on October 7, when it was Hamas that made no distinction between adults and children.

For my entire life, I have stated in every way that to accustom oneself to that outrage, to consider the death of a child as a functional requirement, a statistical datum, a mere detail, is to think like a barbarian.

I think the same thing each time the social networks deliver from Gaza the image of a small, lifeless body pulled from the rubble by his father or mother, or by someone taking their place when they, too, have died.

And I think it no less when the little one is felled by a bullet or bomb or rocket fired by a descendant of the pure souls of the shtetls that the Nazi madness spared from being gassed and burned.

That had to be said.

It had to be clear.

I need no lessons on this subject from those who did not weep with me over the children gassed by Bashar al-Assad in Damascus, the children drowned off the coast of Lampedusa in their open migrant boats, the children bled white in Yemen, Nigeria, or Mogadishu. I will not go on; you get the point.

But what I do want to say is this, and with the utmost emphasis.

The responsibility for these children's deaths lies first and foremost not with Israel but with those who turned them into human shields.

It lies not with the grandchildren of the survivors of Auschwitz, whose searing testimony opened the world's conscience to the outrage of the killing of children, but with the Islamic terrorists who, after years spent indoctrinating their own children in anti-Jewish hate and impressing them into service, hijacking and militarizing their parents, imposing on them a *sharia* ever less spiritual and ever more sadistic, working their people like dough or, more accurately, like a metal with which they would fashion a bomb aimed at Israel and designed explicitly to explode into shards.

The responsibility lies with the terrorists who set up their stores of weapons and ammunition, their barracks and command centers, their firing ranges and training grounds next to mosques, in hospitals and schools, and at the entrances to tunnels dug under the most populous zones of the miniature Leviathan that Gaza had become.

It lies with those who turned a deaf ear when Israel gave families in Gaza City a deadline of twenty-four hours (extended to two days, then three, then a week) before intensifying its strikes on the bases occupied by the pogromists who had just slit the throats of Israeli children or shot them in the face.

It lies with those who forbade compliance with the Israeli ultimatum; stationed pickups at the access to the Salah al-Din road, which Israel was opening for several hours each day to permit evacuations; or simply fired on Gazans who took the risk of disobeying them and, in some documented cases, had to be escorted out under the protection of an IDF unit.

It lies also, by the way, with the Egyptians, who persist in denying entry to Gazans wishing to leave the Strip in advance of the Rafah offensive. Egypt had opened its border to Libyans fleeing Gaddafi's tanks. Erdogan, barbaric as he is, opened Turkey's border to allow Syrian refugees to escape bombardment by

Bashar al-Assad. In every war, in fact, there is always a neighboring state that, however poor, deprived, or prey to its own convulsions, offers temporary shelter to fellow humans in danger of imminent death. Always, that is, except here, except in the case of Egypt, which is standing by, impassive, while its Palestinian neighbors vainly cry out and pound at its door.

I would also add that if there is blame to be shared, it should be shared with the UN functionaries who compounded the problem by claiming that the evacuations were a trap; that the corridors Israel opened to allow noncombatants to find shelter were dead ends. Israel denies it, they said, but it's preparing a one-way evacuation, an undeclared ethnic cleansing, a second Nakba. Those who made such claims have on their hands the blood of the poor souls who listened to them, who believed them, and who stayed as the bombs began to fall.

I know there were young soldiers, nearly children themselves, who, upon entering a neighborhood that presented a fifty-fifty chance of being mined, lost their cool, fired in a panic, and killed unarmed citizens, or as we saw once, hostages who had been awaiting them as saviors.

I do not believe that the IDF has always been exemplary or that mistakes have not been made in the field, as with the World Central Kitchen tragedy, where civilian aid workers were bombed in their clearly marked vehicles. But here, too, it was a mistake (though the cynics will say otherwise), and these sorts of mistakes must be turned over to the appropriate legal authorities for adjudication, by which I mean real and true justice at the hands of the Israeli military and civil authorities: they alone possess the evidence; they alone are implacable when it comes to the death of children.

And perhaps they are more numerous than we think: the strategists, tacticians, staff and field officers who, as an Israeli journalist once implied in an interview with Prime Minister Netanyahu, have trouble sleeping at night and wonder whether they have always and under all circumstances acted as they should with respect to the number and pace of bombings, the reliance on artificial intelligence to guide firing, the use of algorithms for targeting, and now, as this book draws to a close, the battle in Rafah, in the south, where more than a million people had sought refuge and had to be evacuated before combat began. All of that obviously troubles me greatly; the images, when we have images of these things, haunt me; perhaps they haunt the IDF as well.

But there is one point on which "probably" and "perhaps" are inappropriate—because it is a certitude.

This war is a horrific war that the Israelis did not want.

Their enemy is a terrible adversary whose declared aim is to post not only the greatest possible number of Jewish deaths but also the greatest possible number of martyrs on its own side.

These hybrid combatants who hide in tunnels that they do not use to provide shelter to their own people, and who resurface outside buildings full of civilian men, women, and children, expose themselves to IDF soldiers as if to say, "Kill me if you can, but kill them with me, because in so doing you'll be killing children, and by killing children you'll return to being the outrage of the world."

Caught in this trap, the Israelis had but one choice.

Either they could draw back in horror before the human shields, thinking no, we can't...we have to pull out...we're calling it off...

Or, knowing that in so doing they would be handing the victory to Hamas, they could conclude that they did not have the right to act in that way. Israel, as the saying goes, can win many wars, but it will lose only one—the last one.

That said, only one option remains.

That option is to win.

To win because it is a duty to do so.

But to win while taking every possible precaution in order to minimize civilian casualties—which I believe they have done.

In no other war anywhere in the world have we seen as many control rooms where anxious young officers, their eyes glued to a screen, follow the trajectory of the missile they have launched, watching for the appearance of a shadow, a shape, or a silhouette within the frame, with only a few seconds to alter the course of the missile and cause it to land nearby in a patch of rubble or a field, after which a robot's voice announces, "Diverted missile."

In no other war have we seen an army, once a firm deadline has passed, give the occupants a final chance to leave the area by saturating the area with leaflets, texts, phone calls, and empty rockets released by drones—all at the risk of giving enemy combatants time to flee or take cover while depriving themselves of the element of surprise, a strategic and tactical asset in any war.

And never, in any other war, have we seen the equivalent of the MAG, the forensic unit responsible for verifying—usually from a bunker in Tel Aviv but sometimes in real time by officers embedded in operational units—whether issued orders are consistent with the principle of proportionality required by the laws of war, and also by Israeli law.

All civilized armies have such a code.

The American military has just updated its own.

But I know of none more demanding than the *Tohar HaNeshek*, "purity of arms," codified by Israel's pioneers.

I doubt that Israel waited for anyone—the friends who wish it well, the allies that left it alone on the front line of a fight that concerns them as well, or its enemies—to inundate it with pressure, entreaties, and admonitions before choosing to remain true to its code.

That is why it is necessary to repeat this key point over and over against the evangelists of the theology of reprobation that everywhere is replacing the theology of liberation.

The death of civilians in Gaza is not a massacre.

And it is most certainly not a genocide.

And to assert otherwise—to equate IDF soldiers with Nazis driven by pure hatred and bent on annihilating unarmed populations; to fail to recognize the distinction between an Israeli soldier who kills an innocent person without intending to and the SS, which locked children in cattle cars and gassed them upon arrival; to be incapable (or unwilling) to see what distinguishes an errant shot from cold, methodical murder; to scream "IDF fascist–Biden complicit"; to drape Israel in the noxious cloud that has covered the earth since the massacre of Jewish children in the Holocaust—all that is contrary to the facts and the truth. It is an outrage to yesterday's victims, an affront to today's, a gift to the child-killers of Hamas, and an addition to the misery of the world.

13

Lest We Forget Thee

ONE LAST WORD FOR THOSE to whom the name of
Israel matters.

A commentary by Rashi has intrigued me since I
discovered it in 1979, when I was writing *Le Testa-
ment de Dieu.*

Rashi asks why the Torah does not open directly
at chapter 12 of Exodus, where the verse states, "This
month is to be for you the first month, the first month
of your year."

More specifically, he mentions his father, Rabbi
Isaac, whom he quotes as asking, in essence: Why did
Elohim feel the need, instead of beginning with the
Alliance that he had made with his people, to tell us
in detail these stories of night and light, of earth and
sky, of breath hovering over the surface of the waters,

of formlessness and emptiness; why did he need to impress upon us the "power of his acts"?

And he answers with the subtlety that makes him the most Jewish of French geniuses and the most French of Jewish geniuses.

Imagine that the "nations of the world" say to the Hebrews one day, "You are thieves; it is by force that you conquered the land of the people of Canaan." The Hebrews would be right to respond, "All of the land" belonged to the "Holy One, Blessed Is He." It is he who created it and it is he who, "by an act of his will" (today we would say, with full discernment) "gave it to whom he saw fit."

But there is another gloss by Rashi that appears in the margin of the verse in Leviticus where the Hebrews, newly settled on the land they have been given, find themselves threatened (as they will never cease to be by all the prophets) with being "vomited up" by it, as were the peoples who inhabited it before them.

Rashi compares the land to "a prince who is made to eat a disgusting food" that his delicate stomach could not manage to keep down.

And he concludes from this twin gloss—unless I am the one drawing the conclusions—that this land was indeed given to the Jewish people, but on the condition that they not repeat the terrible errors of the Canaanites. It was given with a mission statement, a sort of road map: Do not be a people like the others;

do not build a nation that resembles other nations; while living there, rise to the task he gave you. The Jewish people are the only ones to have accepted those conditions.

I evoke these biblical memories not only because of the premonitory nature of a gloss telling us that Erdogan's Turks, Khamenei's Iranians, Tebboune's Algerians, and Columbia's raging undergraduates were not the first to accuse the Jews of being thieves and to take the side of the eternal Canaanites; but also because these questions were at the heart of nascent Zionism and the debates that animated it.

On one side were those who saw no reason to impose any particular constraints on the revived Jewish nation. They had no desire, having returned at long last to Canaan, to prove themselves particularly exceptional. And they were so exasperated at the idea of having to prove their credentials to other nations that they went so far as to say, with David Ben-Gurion: "I will be proud of Israel when, like every other country in the world, it has its whores, con men, and gangsters."

Against this group stood other Zionists, who were often members of the first group as well; people who, in their heart of hearts, their pioneering and poetic hearts, their dreaming hearts, had spent their childhood in a shtetl or a ghetto remembering Psalm 126 and giving thanks for the wheat, barley, and yeast they had just eaten. This second group was not sure whether it was worth the trouble to gather the Jewish people together, to revive the Hebrew language, and to make the immense effort to make the desert bloom if it was just to create one more nation, one more state, one more cold monster resembling all the other cold monsters.

A refuge, of course, where the oldest persecuted people in the world would have the right to live without being slaves, serfs, muzhiks; subhuman and untouchable; fearing at any moment the appearance of the knife or pitchfork that would tear their belly open.

A state for survivors of the Holocaust, obviously, in which one would no longer be the being-for-death, the being-for-massacre, the lamb on the butcher's block, the child's flesh in the crematorium, disappearing in a plume of smoke and ash.

But this group of Zionists also thought the following: Maybe it is a blessing to have waited so long and been the latecomer to the concert of nations that was blown in on the wind of the French Revolution. Let's make an opportunity out of being one of the last bursts in the great explosion of national movements by which the peoples of the world sought to emancipate themselves from kings and empires. And let's use the timing to avoid the childhood illnesses that other nations have suffered through.

Arrogance, for example.

The self-satisfaction of those who feel they have all the rights, including the right to say to others around them or among them: This land is mine, unconditionally mine—clear out so that I can get started!

The chauvinism that Romain Gary, odd Jew that he was, described so well in his famous observation: Patriotism is love for one's own; chauvinism and nationalism are hate for others.

In a word, why not create a Jewish state, simply Jewish, where one would be both "resident and foreigner," at home while also visiting? Why not try, as Rashi recommended, to inhabit the land with a light touch, to sanctify it without idolizing it, to occupy it like a guest whose mission is to sow and harvest while leaving to the trees the business of putting down roots?

If only that had been asked of all the world's nations!

It was asked of the renascent Jewish nation—and it was done.

Now, if we place the real Israel of today side by side with the original project, what do we see? Has the Jewish state adhered to its program?

In the government, I see two men whose names burn my tongue. One, Bezalel Smotrich, defines himself as a "fascist homophobe" who encourages "punitive expeditions" in the villages of the West Bank and preaches "emigration" of all Gazans. The other,

Itamar Ben-Gvir, calls himself not a Canaanite but a Kahanist, a disciple of Meir Kahane, the Brooklyn-born rabbi who, before his party was banned in 1994 for terrorism and racism, advocated depriving Arab Israelis of the right to vote and expelling them from the country.

I see a prime minister, Benjamin Netanyahu, who—perhaps to please these two, perhaps for base political reasons, perhaps because he feels his time is coming to an end, or perhaps, alas, because he has served one term too many and has lost his Jewish compass—was busy before the war undermining a judicial system that has been the pride of Israel. With all its qualms and uncertainties, with the renewal, deepening, and continuous reinvention of its laws, with the limits it places on the hubris of cynical actors, isn't democracy the least bad secular translation of the instruction given to the people of Israel to remain a just people?

I see Jewish activists who, in the fog of war, are pursuing settlements in the West Bank, substantial ones that undermine the existence of a viable Palestinian state, with which one day Israel is simply going to have to come to terms if it wants to inhabit the land as Rashi recommended—and to make peace.

I see Jews in Israel and Europe who, sickened by the attacks upon them by those they had considered their allies, exhausted by their sudden unexpected isolation, are listening to bad shepherds who tell them:

"We need to leave behind the world of the gentle men who have repaid us so badly for having, in two or three lifetimes, revived the flame that lit the fire of three of the greatest civilizations in the world."

I know these errant counselors. I know that the grace of the Jewish path in the world is the absolute opposite of the one they are urging. And I would like to be able to convince those tempted to follow their bad guidance that the history of Israel, the political experience of Israel, the adventure of its generals and kings, the glory of Gideon and of Menachem (Begin), the dreams of Joshua and of Shimon (Peres), Yitzhak (Rabin and Shamir), Ehud (Barak), and Golda (Meir) are the radical, unassailable, and definitive negation of the chauvinism and populism that are gaining ground in much of the world today.

"Make us a golden calf," demanded the Israelites; make us a god who will march before us; make us an idol that will spare us the effort of thinking. So today speak those Jews who wish to consign their soul to the false friends of the people.

Take us back into Egypt, grumbled the assembled tribes of Israel to Moses and Aaron, for at least there we were seated "near pots of meat" and "ate bread until we were full." The tendency to become a flock of followers, passive and self-indulgent, is the temptation of all peoples. But is it not a threat to the new rendition of the world's most ancient people that Israel aspires to become?

The prophets were not wrong in speaking of the immense effort it takes to shape a people.

They knew that nothing is more resistant to intelligence, truth, and transcendence than a body of people, any people, including those of Israel.

They knew that Jewish thought is a fountain of meaning and not one drop must be lost. Each pearl is the rarest of essences and the most precious of nectars, and of which sometimes even the Jews want no more to drink.

And I see that many Jews today would willingly unburden themselves, if they could, of the greatness of Israel.

And then I see the remainder.

I do not mean "what remains of Israel."

Not the "remainder" that, in the Bible, is left on the ground when the harvest is ruined and all seems lost.

No.

I see the brave young and not-so-young soldiers on the northern border, waiting stoically for the hellfire promised by Hezbollah and its Iranian sponsor.

I see the people united around the hostages, united as on the first day, those who have recovered theirs and those who have lost hope; those who know that theirs will never return but, having mourned, gather in support of those still waiting. There they are, tense and grave, exchanging bits of news and trying to imagine the rest: The filth...the vermin.... Are our people being fed?.... Can they sleep? The same bowl for washing and eating.... The mud of the tunnel or, contrarily, its clean, icy floor.... An old newspaper the only reading material.... The swaggering guards who make a game of frightening their charges.... Death.... Do we even know how many are already gone? And the sexual violence, the rapes, women treated as slaves or cattle.... They are gathered as one and agree on this point of Jewish doctrine: Nothing is worth more than a life; no political or geopolitical consideration, no calculation, can or should stand against the obligation to bring the captives back; the war can only end, and be won, when the hostages come home.

I walk through a Tel Aviv petrified but still so vibrant, its society composed of Sephardic and Ashkenazi citizens, of ultra-modern start-uppers and ultra-archaic religious spirits from Poland, of seculars, half-Ukrainian and half-Californian, of Arab Israelis, Black Israelis, Druze.

Tomorrow, I am going to Jerusalem. There, I will see rabbis and bishops, Armenian monks and Catholic nuns, studious young people in black hats, ageless Hasidim clothed in fur despite the heat. They will be like a waltz of people spinning through the hilly landscape. As the murmur of the Book that we never tire of questioning streams through the open windows of the yeshivas, the dancers will know not where they are, with whom, or in what era. All they will know is that they have received a land, and that they are to work and build and transform its arid expanses into gardens. And they know that one thing, just one, is forbidden: presumptuousness, immodesty, and overweening pride are the cancer of nations.

And then I will return to the kibbutzim. The descendants of the pioneers who had made the voyage to the last circle of hell.... The physicians, lawyers, intellectuals, and engineers who, after working in the fields, hurried back to their libraries, their reading glasses, and, as in the novels of Amos Oz, their tales of love and darkness.... And then the horror, the carnage, door to door, one by one, the stampede of pogromists.... And where, like the boy in Roman Vishniac's famous photo, scrutinizing the corner of a building to see if the killers have gone, the survivors of October 7 are beginning to come back.

I love this little world of people stranded on the tiny strip of land they finally received, three-quarters of a century ago, left there by a West and by a larger world wet with the rivers of Jewish blood spilled into the torrent of centuries.

I love the fact that, faced with the mixed blessing that a flesh-and-blood nation can be, faced with the poison apple of a state that it received, like Snow

White, from queens and kings hoping thus to be even after centuries of persecution, Israel conserved the subtle ability to siphon from it the poison of chauvinism and, like fire-breathers, sometimes *in extremis*, cast it away.

And I love this miracle of endurance and intelligence, lucidity and goodness: As on the first day, exactly as on the first day, when they heard their neighbors calling for their death and the destruction of their nation, the Israelis remain, for the most part, faithful to their founding principles and receptive to peace—as soon as the others are too.

That is a living Zionism.

That is a radiant, luminous, exemplary Zionism.

Perhaps it is now less widely shared than I believe.

But it is exemplary because, despite wars, despite blows administered and blows received, it holds fast to Abraham's commandment: "This house that we have built" should be "a house of prayer for all peoples."

Let those who disagree with that say so.

In so doing, they will simply be saying that they hate people.

For a long time, exiled Jews chanted, their harps hung from a tree in a sign of sadness, "If I forget thee, Jerusalem, may my hand wither."

Today, perhaps Israel's Jews should chant: If I forget thee, Jewish soul…

If I forget thee, sacred voice whispering that saving a life is worth more than observing all the Shabbats in the world…

If I forget thee, soul of a people that has always placed spirit over faith and the letter over spirit…

If I forget thee, irremediable and noble fragility (for spirit is fragile, intelligence is fragile, humanity is fragile) that is not the opposite of strength but rather keeps strength from being barbarous…

If I forget thee, Jewish existence that has overcome so many tests, survived so many massacres, and never lost its detachment from the powers that be nor its ironic stance toward self-styled greatness…

If I forget thee, Jewish solitude, the other, true form of solitude, which allowed Abraham, just and first among Adams, to stand on the riverbank, as the Midrash tells us, while the peoples of history stood on the other side…

If I forget thee, admirable Rabbis who, in the shadow of the gallows, before the butchers of the Inquisition, at the gate to the gas chamber, have borne consistent witness that one can be in history while being out of it, in time and beyond time, for there is an "other than being"…

If I forget thee, Jewish exception that sought with all its strength to save the Name…

If I forget thee, Jewish responsibility inscribed in the Talmud with the words: "All Jews are the guarantors, one and all," and if I forget thee, Jewish super-respon-sibility that reminded a Jewish prime minister that though the murder of the children of Israel is unpar-donable, more unpardonable still is to force Israel to kill the children of murderers...

If I forget thee, Jewish humanism...

If I forget thee, hope, in Benny Lévy's account, drawing Sartre to Judaism...

If I forget thee, Adam, name of the man who survived the waves of time, which, like the sea, erases all...

If I forget thee, promise recalled, now and forever, to men and women who are born, live, and die solely in time...

That day has not come.

We have not forgotten.

The soul, mind, and genius of Judaism are standing firm amid tumult and torment.

But if we forget them, it is not the hand of Israel that will wither, but its heart.

Notes

PART ONE

Page 12. "…Valdai Discussion Club…"

Uliana Pavlova, Sugam Pokharel, and Amy Cassidy, "Putin Accuses Western Elites of Playing 'Dangerous, Bloody and Dirty Game,'" CNN, October 27, 2022, https://www.cnn.com/2022/10/27/europe/russia-vladimir-putin-valdai-club-speech-intl/index.html.

Page 13. "…Aleksandr Dugin…"

The Nexus Institute, "Bernard-Henri Lévy vs. Aleksandr Dugin at the Nexus Symposium 2019," October 11, 2019, YouTube video, https://www.youtube.com/watch?v=x70z5QWC9qs.

Page 13. "A BBC analysis…"

Abdelali Ragad, Richard Irvine-Brown, Benedict Garman, and Sean Seddon, "How Hamas Built a Force to Attack Israel on 7 October," BBC, November 27, 2023, https://www.bbc.com/news/world-middle-east-67480680.

Page 15. "…yes, there were beaches…"

Sara Serfaty, "Gaza Beaches Made Safe for Swimming with Help of Environmental Peace Group," *The Times of Israel*, June 10, 2022, https://www.timesofisrael.com/gaza-beaches-made-safe-for-swimming-with-help-of-environmental-peace-group/; Nidal Al-Mughrabi, "For the First Time in Years, Gazans Enjoy Clean Seawater," Reuters, June 9, 2022, https://www.reuters.com/world/middle-east/first-time-years-gazans-enjoy-clean-seawater-2022-06-09/.

Page 15. "...yes, there were five-star hotels in Gaza..."

Harriet Sherwood, "Gaza's First Five-Star Hotel Provides Luxury and Hope Amid the Blockades," *The Guardian*, August 8, 2011, https://www.theguardian.com/world/2011/aug/08/gaza-first-five-star-hotel.

Page 15. "...brain cancer..."

Nathan Rennolds, "Israeli Doctors Saved the Life of Hamas Leader, Whom They Now Blame for the October 7 Terrorist Attacks, When He Was in Prison, Reports Say," *Business Insider*, October 22, 2023, https://www.businessinsider.com/hamas-gaza-leader-survived-tumor-operation-israel-reports-2023-10.

Page 32. "...the New York Times's long investigation..."

Jeffrey Gettleman, Anat Schwartz, and Adam Sella, "'Screams Without Words': How Hamas Weaponized Sexual Violence on Oct. 7," *The New York Times*, March 25, 2024, https://www.nytimes.com/2023/12/28/world/middleeast/oct-7-attacks-hamas-israel-sexual-violence.html.

Page 33. "I killed ten...ten with my own hands...."

"Army Publishes Audio of Hamas Terrorist Calling Parents to Brag of Killing Jews," *The Times of Israel*, October 24, 2023, https://www.timesofisrael.com/liveblog_entry/army-publishes-audio-of-hamas-terrorist-calling-parents-to-brag-of-killing-jews/; Stewart Bell, "In Phone Recording Found After Hamas Attack Son Tells Parents He 'Killed Jews,'" *Global News*, October 24, 2023, https://globalnews.ca/news/10046530/israel-call-your-son-killed-jews/.

Page 36. "The Empire of Hamas."

Lee Smith, "The Global Empire of Palestine," Tablet, December 19, 2023, https://www.tabletmag.com/sections/news/articles/global-empire-of-palestine.

Page 39. "It was clear with respect to Turkish President Erdogan…"

Lazar Berman, "Erdogan: Hamas Are Not Terrorists; They Are Mujahideen Defending Their Homeland," *The Times of Israel*, October 25, 2023, https://fr.timesofisrael.com/erdogan-le-hamas-nest-pas-terroriste-ce-sont-des-moudjahidines-qui-defendent-leur-patrie/; Ben Hubbard and Safak Timur, "Turkey's Leader, Lashing Out at Israel, Defends Hamas," *The New York Times*, October 25, 2023, https://www.nytimes.com/2023/10/25/world/middleeast/erdogan-turkey-hamas-israel.html.

Page 39. "We saw him, his neck wrapped in a Palestinian keffiyeh…"

Nicolas Bourcier, "Turkish President Erdogan Champions the Palestinian Cause, Fiercely Attacks Israel," *Le Monde*, October 30, 2023, https://www.lemonde.fr/international/article/2023/10/29/en-turquie-le-president-erdogan-se-fait-champion-de-la-cause-palestinienne-et-attaque-violemment-israel_6197060_3210.html.

Page 39. "…compared Bibi Netanyahu to Hitler…"

Nadav Gavrielov and Safak Timur, "Erdogan Compares Netanyahu to Hitler," *The New York Times*, December 27, 2023, https://www.nytimes.com/2023/12/27/world/middleeast/erdogan-turkey-netanyahu-hitler.html.

Page 40. "Iran began with denial…"

"The Head of Hezbollah Met with Leaders of Hamas and Islamic Jihad," *L'Opinion*, October 25, 2023, https://www.lopinion.fr/international/le-chef-du-hezbollah-a-rencontre-des-dirigeants-du-hamas-et-du-djihad-islamique.

Marianne Max, "'We Are Not Afraid of Anyone': This Iranian Minister Admits to Having Helped Hamas," *Watson*, November 29, 2023, https://www.watson.ch/fr/international/israel/630651190-un-ministre-iranien-avoue-avoir-aide-le-hamas.

Baybars Can, "Iranian Deputy Foreign Minister Meets with a Hamas Delegation in Moscow," *AA*, October 27, 2023, https://www.aa.com.tr/fr/monde/le-vice-ministre-iranien-des-affaires-étrangères-rencontre-une-délégation-du-hamas-à-moscou-/3034496.

Reuters, "The Leader of Hamas Met with the Iranian Supreme Leader-Hamas," *Challenges*, April 11, 2023, https://www.challenges.fr/top-news/le-chef-du-hamas-a-rencontre-le-guide-supreme-iranien-hamas_872974.

"Seen from the United States. Hamas Attack: Iran's (In)Visible Hand," *Courrier International*, October 9, 2023, https://www.courrierinternational.com/article/vu-des-etats-unis-operation-du-hamas-la-main-in-visible-de-l-iran.

Summer Said, Dov Lieber, and Benoit Faucon, "Hamas Fighters Trained in Iran Before Oct. 7 Attacks," *The Wall Street Journal*, October 25, 2023, https://www.wsj.com/world/middle-east/hamas-fighters-trained-in-iran-before-oct-7-attacks-e2a8dbb9.

Page 42. "…that fateful moment…"

Jordyn Haime, "China: Since the October 7 Massacre in Hamas, Anti-Semitism Has Exploded Online," *The Times of Israel*, November 11, 2023, https://fr.timesofisrael.com/chine-depuis-le-massacre-du-7-octobre-au-hamas-lantisemitisme-a-explose-en-ligne/.

Page 42. "…the icing on the cake was Putin."

Martin Küper, "Putin Reportedly Used Hamas to Trap Ukraine," *Watson*, October 10, 2023, https://www.watson.ch/fr/international/guerre/733655863 poutine aurait vendu des armes au-hamas-et-accuse-l-ukraine.

Page 43. "…Hamas leaders had two sessions with Russian Foreign Minister Sergey Lavrov…"

TOI Staff, "Russia's Lavrov Meets with Hamas Politburo Chief Haniyeh in Moscow," *The Times of Israel*, September 13, 2022, https://www.timesofisrael.com/russias-lavrov-meets-with-hamas-politburo-chief-haniyeh-in-moscow/.

Beatrice Farhat, "Hamas Says Leadership Visited Russia, Met Sergey Lavrov," *Al-Monitor*, March 14, 2023, https://www. al-monitor.com/originals/2023/03/hamas-says-leadership-visited-russia-met-sergey-lavrov.

PART TWO

Page 49. "About the reality of the acts..."

Joseph Confavreux, "The October 7 Operation Is Not Only Aimed at Killing, but at Filming Killings and Atrocities," *MediaPart*, November 21, 2023, https://www.mediapart.fr/journal/inter national/211123/l-operation-du-7-octobre-ne-vise-pas-seulement-tuer-mais-filmer-les-tueries-et-les-atrocites.

Page 50. "We watched as New York Congressman Jamaal Bowman..."

Carl Campanile, "'Squad' Member Jamaal Bowman Calls Israel an 'Apartheid' State, Reported Rapes Were a 'Lie': Video," *New York Post*, March 26, 2024, https://nypost.com/2024/03/26/us-news/squad-member-jamaal-bowman-calls-israel-an-apart-heid-state-reported-rapes-were-a-lie-video/.

Page 51. "We watched as an adviser..."

Hannah Gillott and Jane Prinsley, "Outrage as Foreign Office Sexual Violence Adviser Backs Claim that Israel Lied About Rapes," *The Jewish Chronicle*, January 18, 2024, https://www. thejc.com/news/uk/deep-concern-over-anti-israel-culture-at-foreign-office-ykrgqr0o.

Nicole Lampert, "MeToo Unless You're a Jew," *UnHerd*, November 17, 2023, https://unherd.com/2023/11/metoo-unless-youre-a-jew/.

Page 53. "We saw Rep. Rashida Tlaib of Michigan..."

Juliette Kayyem, "Rashida Tlaib's Inflammatory Language," *The Atlantic*, November 8, 2023, https://www.theatlantic.com/ideas/archive/2023/11/rashida-tlaib-congress-palestinian-resistance-river-to-sea/675932/.

"United States. Rashida Tlaib, Spokesperson for the Palestinians at the Washington Congress," *Courrier International*, December 23, 2023, https://www.courrierinternational.com/article/etats-unis-rashida-tlaib-porte-voix-des-palestiniens-au-congres-de-washington.

"Rashida Tlaib Is Part of a Secret Group on the Networks that Glorifies Hamas," *i24 News*, November 15, 2023, https://www.i24news.tv/fr/actu/israel-en-guerre/1700051674-rashi-da-tlaib-fait-partie-d-un-groupe-secret-sur-les-reseaux-qui-glorifie-le-hamas.

Page 53. "Bowman, who later cast doubt on the rape allegations…"

https://www.politico.com/live-updates/2024/03/26/congress/bowman-house-israel-october-7-sexual-assault-hamas-00148426.

Page 54. "…the Democratic Socialists of America…"

Joshua Solomon, "Top N.Y. Lawmakers Denounce Pro-Palestinian Times Square Rally," *Times Union*, October 9, 2023, https://www.timesunion.com/state/article/hochul-dems-denounce-pro-palestine-times-square-18415341.php.

Page 55. "The Red Cross led the way…"

Roni Rabin, "Hamas Hostages and Families of Captives Sue Red Cross in Israeli Court," *The New York Times*, December 22, 2023, https://www.nytimes.com/2023/12/22/world/middle east/israel-hamas-hostages-red-cross-lawsuit.html.

Itamar Eichner, "Released Hamas Hostage Raz Ben Ami Is Suing the Red Cross: 'It Doesn't Care About Hostages,'" *Ynetnews*, December 21, 2023, https://www.ynetnews.com/article/ryiqd 00zvt.

Isabel Keane, "Daughter of Critically Ill Freed Hostage Rips Red Cross: 'Medically Neglected,'" *New York Post*, November 27, 2023, https://nypost.com/2023/11/27/news/daughter-of-critically-ill-freed-hostage-rips-red-cross-medically-neglected/.

Page 57. "...Secretary General António Guterres set the tone..."

António Guterres, "Secretary-General's Remarks to the Press on the Situation in the Middle East," United Nations, October 9, 2023, https://www.un.org/sg/en/content/sg/speeches/2023-10-09/secretary-generals-remarks-the-press-the-situation-the-middle-east.

Page 58. "...rapporteur for human rights in the occupied Palestinian territories."

Mike Wagenheim, "'An Illegitimate Act of Resistance Does Not Delegitimize Resistance,' UN Special Rapporteur Tells i24NEWS," *i24 News*, December 23, 2023, https://www.i24news.tv/fr/actu/israel-en-guerre/1702547743-un-acte-de-resistance-illegitime-ne-delegitime-pas-la-resistance-declare-le-rapporteur-special-de-l-onu-a-i24news.

Page 58. "...in a report entitled 'Anatomy of Genocide'..."

Human Rights Council, "Rights Expert Finds 'Reasonable Grounds' Genocide Is Being Committed in Gaza," United Nations, March 26, 2024, https://news.un.org/en/story/2024/03/1147976.

Page 58. "...its deputy head, Sarah Douglas, posed in front of a Palestinian flag..."

The Editorial Board, "Hamas's Friends at the United Nations," *The Wall Street Journal*, December 20, 2023, https://www.wsj.com/articles/united-nations-hamas-israel-gaza-alice-wairimu-nderitu-sarah-douglas-cindy-mccain-260ea505.

Page 58. "...Pramila Patten, Special Representative of the Secretary-General on Sexual Violence..."

Office of the Special Representative of the Secretary-General, "Sexual Violence in Conflict," Press Release, United Nations, March 4, 2024, https://www.un.org/sexualviolenceinconflict/press-release/israel-west-bank-mission/.

Page 59. "…UN Women brought up this report…"

UN Women Executive Director Sima Bahous, "Speech: 'We Can and Must Choose to End Poverty for Women and Girls,'" UN Women, March 11, 2024, https://www.unwomen.org/en/news-stories/speech/2024/03/speech-we-can-and-must-choose-to-end-poverty-for-women-and-girls.

Page 59. "…there were vehement protests within the UN…"

Ali Abunimah, "Why Does the UN Office for the Prevention of Genocide Remain Silent About Gaza?" Charleroi pour la Palestine, December 14, 2023, https://charleroi-pourla palestine.be/index.php/2023/12/14/pourquoi-le-bureau-de-lonu-pour-la-prevention-de-genocide-reste-t-il-silencieux-a-propos-de-gaza/.

David Charter and Will Pavia, "UN Genocide Adviser Urged to Quit Over Israel Stance," *The Times*, December 21, 2023, https://www.thetimes.co.uk/article/un-genocide-adviser-urged-to-quit-over-israel-stance-lxwzgvcct.

Page 60. "Cindy McCain…"

Helen Murphy, "Devex Newswire: Cindy McCain's Tearful Clash with WFP Staff Over Gaza," *Devex*, December 1, 2023, https://www.devex.com/news/devex-newswire-cindy-mccain-s-tearful-clash-with-wfp-staff-over-gaza-106701.

Page 60. "And let us not forget UNRWA…"

"IDF Finds Terrorist Vests Hidden in UNRWA Bags in Gaza Clinic," *i24 News*, January 6, 2024, https://www.i24news.tv/en/news/israel-at-war/1704531904-idf-finds-terrorist-vests-hidden-in-unrwa-bags-in-gaza-clinic.

Benny Avni, "UN Agency in Gaza Alleged to Have 'Blood on Its Hands' in Aftermath of October 7 Massacre of Israelis," *The New York Sun*, January 24, 2024, https://www.nysun.com/article/un-agency-in-gaza-alleged-to-have-blood-on-its-hands-in-aftermath-of-october-7-massacre-of-israelis.

The World with AFP, "Israel-Hamas War: UNRWA Separates from 'Several' of Its Employees, Suspected of Having Participated in the October 7 Attack," *Le Monde*, January 26, 2024, https://www.lemonde.fr/international/article/2024/01/26/guerre-israel-hamas-l-unrwa-se-separe-de-plusieurs-de-ses-employes-soupconnes-d-avoir-participe-a-l-attaque-du-7-octobre_6213217_3210.html.

Jeremy Sharon, "UNRWA Employees Praised the Hamas Massacres: IMPACT-se Study," *The Times of Israel*, November 6, 2023, https://fr.timesofisrael.com/des-employes-de-lunrwa-ont-fait-leloge-des-massacres-du-hamas-etude-impact-se/.

Patricia Zengerle, "US Congress Deal Bars US Funds to UNRWA Until March 2025, Sources Say," Reuters, March 19, 2024, https://www.reuters.com/world/us/us-congress-deal-bars-us-funds-unrwa-until-march-2025-sources-say-2024-03-19/.

Tim Stickings and Sunniva Rose, "Which Countries Have Resumed Funding to UNRWA in Gaza?" *The National News*, March 29, 2024, https://www.thenationalnews.com/news/mena/2024/03/30/which-countries-have-resumed-funding-to-unrwa-in-gaza/.

Page 61. "...*the announcement that Iran had assumed the presidency...*"

Emma Farge, "Iran's Appointment to Chair UN Rights Meeting Draws Condemnation," Reuters, November 2, 2023, https://www.reuters.com/world/irans-appointment-chair-un-rights-meeting-draws-condemnation-2023-11-02/.

Vivan Nereim, "Saudi Arabia, Lagging on Women's Rights, Is to Lead U.N. Women's Forum," *The New York Times*, March 28, 2024, https://www.nytimes.com/2024/03/28/world/middleeast/saudi-arabia-un-women.html.

Page 69. "*First, if we are talking about a true ceasefire...*"

Nidal Al-Mughrabi, "Hamas Rejects Israel's Ceasefire Response, Sticks to Main Demands," Reuters, April 13, 2024, https://www.reuters.com/world/middle-east/hamas-rejects-israels-ceasefire-response-sticks-main-demands-2024-04-13/.

Page 71. "...a father who had buried his son..."

Isabel Keane, "Israeli Father Says Hamas Tried to Sell His Son's Decapitated Head for $10,000," *New York Post*, January 17, 2024, https://nypost.com/2024/01/17/news/israeli-dad-says-hamas-tried-to-sell-sons-decapitated-head/.

Page 73. "...then rest assured..."

Zach Kessel, "National-Security Experts Unveil 'Day After' Plan for Post-War Gaza," *National Review*, March 1, 2024, https://www.nationalreview.com/news/national-security-experts-unveil-day-after-plan-for-post-war-gaza/.

Bret Stephens, "An Arab Mandate for Palestine," *The New York Times*, March 19, 2024, https://www.nytimes.com/2024/03/19/opinion/gaza-war-palestine-arab-mandate.html.

Page 73. "But a plan was nonetheless proposed..."

Wyre Davies and Alys Davies, "Israel-Gaza War: What Is Tel Aviv's Plan for the Strip After the War?" BBC, January 14, 2024, https://www.bbc.com/afrique/monde-67902844.

Haley Ott, "Israeli Defense Minister Lays Out Vision for Post-War Gaza," CBS News, January 5, 2024, https://www.cbsnews.com/news/israeli-gaza-gallant-plan-post-war-hamas/.

Page 81. "...the number of anti-Semitic acts..."

Emma Ferrand, Jeanne Paturaud, and Paul-Henri Wallet, "'Death to the Jews': At Nanterre University, Anti-Semitism Prospers," *Le Figaro*, November 17, 2023, https://www.lefigaro.fr/actualite-france/mort-aux-juifs-a-la-fac-de-nanterre-l-antisemitisme-prospere-20231117.

Abel Quentin, "Abel Quentin: Threatened Like a Jew in France,'" *Marianne*, October 27, 2023, https://www.marianne.net/agora/humeurs/abel-quentin-menace-comme-un-juif-en-france.

Page 82. "...sites for the spray-painting of swastikas..."

Soazig The Nevé, "The Shadow of Anti-Semitism Fractures the Student Community in Universities," *Le Monde*, December 1, 2023, https://www.lemonde.fr/societe/article/2023/12/01/a-l-universite-l-ombre-de-l-antisemitisme-fracture-la-communaute-etudiante_6203293_3224.html.

NOTES

Page 82. "I keep a close eye on Mr. Mélenchon."

Sandrine Cassini, "Anti-Semitism: Jean-Luc Mélenchon's Choice of Ambiguity," *Le Monde*, January 8, 2024, https://www.lemonde.fr/en/france/article/2024/01/08/anti-semitism-jean-luc-melenchon-s-choice-of-ambiguity_6413685_7.html.

Page 83. "...demonstrations of support for 'Palestine'..."

Patrick Reilly, "Pro-Palestinian Protesters Shut Down Grand Central Terminal During Evening Rush," *New York Post*, October 27, 2023, https://nypost.com/2023/10/27/metro/pro-palestinian-protesters-shut-down-grand-central-terminal-during-evening-rush/.

Larry Celona, Georgia Worrell, Valentina Jaramillo, et al., "7,000 Pro-Palestinian Protesters Take Over Brooklyn Bridge, Call for Elimination of Jewish State: 'By Any Means,'" *New York Post*, October 28, 2023, https://nypost.com/2023/10/28/metro/9k-pro-palestinian-protestors-take-over-brooklyn-bridge-call-for-elimination-of-jewish-state-by-any-means/.

Josh Marcus, "Pro-Palestine Protesters Cause Havoc, Closing Down Golden Gate Bridge and Brooklyn Bridge," *The Independent*, April 15, 2024, https://www.yahoo.com/news/pro-palestine-protesters-cause-havoc-233605027.html.

Eyewitness News, "Pro-Palestinian Protesters Deface Front of the New York City Public Library," ABC, November 23, 2023, https://abc7ny.com/nyc-public-library-pro-palestinian-protest-midtown-demonstration/14097280/.

Edward Helmore, "'No Xmas as Usual': Pro-Palestinian Protesters Demonstrate in US Cities," *The Guardian*, December 24, 2023, https://www.theguardian.com/world/2023/dec/24/pro-palestinian-marches-us-cities-christmas.

Tara Suter, "'No Christmas as Usual,': Pro-Palestinian Protesters Storm City Streets on 'Super Saturday,'" *The Hill*, December 23, 2023, https://thehill.com/policy/international/4375545-no-christmas-as-usual-pro-palestinian-protestors-storm-city-streets-on-super-saturday/.

Jesse O'Neill and Carl Campanile, "Pro-Palestinian Group Shares 'Reprehensible' Antisemitic Map of NYC Targets on Social Media," *New York Post*, November 16, 2023, https://nypost.com/2023/11/16/metro/pro-palestinian-group-shares-reprehensible-antisemitic-map-of-nyc-targets-on-social-media/.

Luke Tress, "US Pro-Palestinian Group Blasted for Map of Jewish Groups with 'Blood on Their Hands,'" *The Times of Israel*, November 17, 2023, https://www.timesofisrael.com/us-pro-palestinian-group-blasted-for-map-of-jewish-groups-with-blood-on-their-hands/.

Page 84. "…the mudslide that occurred…"

Sofia Rubinson, "Cornell Professor 'Exhilarated' by Hamas's Attack Defends Remark," *The Cornell Daily Sun*, October 16, 2023, https://cornellsun.com/2023/10/16/cornell-professor-exhilarated-by-hamass-attack-defends-remark/.

"Hamas-Israel War: A Student Arrested in New York for Threats to Jewish Comrades," *20 Minutes*, January 11, 2023, https://www.20minutes.fr/monde/4060399-20231101-guerre-hamas-israel-etudiant-arrete-new-york-menaces-visant-camarades-juifs.

Page 84. "…music festival deserve what happened…"

Alan Johnson, "'Progressives' and the Hamas Pogrom: An A-Z Guide," *Fathom Journal*, October 9, 2023, https://fathomjournal.org/progressives-and-the-hamas-pogrom-an-a-z-guide/.

"The Rave Party of October 7, a 'Provocation,' According to a French Vice-Admiral," *The Times of Israel*, December 30, 2023, https://fr.timesofisrael.com/la-rave-party-du-7-octobre-une-provocation-selon-un-vice-amiral-francais/.

Page 85. "At Cooper Union…"

Louis Keene, "Jewish Students at Cooper Union Told to Hide as Pro-Palestinian Protesters Banged on Doors of Locked Library," *The Forward*, October 25, 2023, https://forward.com/fast-forward/566967/cooper-union-library-jewish-students-hide-protest/.

NOTES

Alan Johnson, "'Progressives' and the Hamas Pogrom: An A-Z Guide," *Fathom Journal*, October 9, 2023, https://fathomjournal.org/progressives-and-the-hamas-pogrom-an-a-z-guide/.

Anel Fajardo, "Antisemitism at Rutgers University: An Open Letter from Rutgers Faculty and Staff," *The Gleaner*, December 8, 2023, https://gleaner.rutgers.edu/2023/12/08/antisemitism-at-rutgers-university-an-open-letter-from-rutgers-faculty-and-staff/.

Page 85. "...the presidents of Harvard, MIT, and Penn..."

Leila Fadel, "After Penn, Members of Congress Call for Harvard and MIT Presidents to Resign," *Morning Edition*, NPR, December 11, 2023, https://www.npr.org/2023/12/11/1218495642/after-penn-calls-for-harvard-and-mit-presidents-to-resign-grow.

College Pulse and FIRE, "2024 College Free Speech Rankings: What Is the State of Free Speech on America's College Campuses?" https://www.thefire.org/sites/default/files/2023/09/CFSR%202024_final_updated.pdf.

Pierre Valentin, "Resignation of the President of Harvard: The Trompe-l'Oeil Defeat of Wokism," *Le Point*, May 1, 2024, https://www.lepoint.fr/postillon/demission-de-la-presidente-de-harvard-la-defaite-en-trompe-l-oeil-du-wokisme-05-01-2024-2549056_3961.php#11.

Page 85. "...the campus was transformed..."

Brie Stimson, "Anti-Israel Protesters Heard Shouting 'We Are Hamas,' 'Long Live Hamas,' Amid Columbia U Demonstrations," Fox News, April 19, 2024, https://www.foxnews.com/us/anti-israel-protesters-heard-shouting-we-hamas-long-live-hamas-columbia-university-demonstrations.

Damita Menezes, Rich McHugh, Urja Sinha, "Pro-Palestine Protesters at Columbia Call for 'Total Divestment,'" *News Nation*, April 23, 2024, https://www.newsnationnow.com/world/israel-palestine/rabbi-columbia-student-protest-antisemitism/.

Michael Koh, "UNC Students for Justice in Palestine Organize Protest in Support of Columbia Students," *Chapelboro.com*, April 19, 2024, https://chapelboro.com/news/unc-students-for-justice-in-palestine-organize-protest-in-support-of-columbia-students.

"Pro-Divestment Protesters Stay Overnight on Beinecke Plaza, No Arrests," *Yale Daily News*, April 19, 2024, https://yaledailynews.com/blog/2024/04/19/about-400-gather-on-beinecke-plaza-to-demand-that-yale-divest-from-military-weapons-manufacturers/.

Valentina Jaramillo and Jorge Fitz-Gibbon, "New School Students Hijack Lobby with Anti-Israel Tent City in Solidarity with Columbia 'Comrades,'" *New York Post*, April 21, 2024, https://nypost.com/2024/04/21/us-news/new-school-students-hijack-lobby-with-anti-israel-tent-city-in-solidarity-with-columbia-comrades/.

Page 90. *"And what of Jordan Bardella…"*

Clément Guillou, "Jordan Bardella Denies Jean-Marie Le Pen's Anti-Semitism and Re-Demonizes the National Rally," *Le Monde*, November 6, 2023, https://www.lemonde.fr/politique/article/2023/11/06/bardella-nie-l-antisemitisme-de-jean-marie-le-pen-et-rediabolise-le-rassemblement-national_6198584_823448.html.

Page 91. *"And what of Donald Trump himself…"*

Ryan Cooper, "What Donald Trump Has Said About Jews," *The Week*, April 18, 2019, https://theweek.com/articles/835714/what-donald-trump-said-about-jews.

Page 91. *"Then there is Viktor Orbán…"*

Bernard-Henri Lévy, "How an Anti-Totalitarian Militant Discovered Ultranationalism," *The Atlantic*, May 13, 2019, https://www.theatlantic.com/ideas/archive/2019/05/bernard-henri-levy-interviews-viktor-orban/589102/.

NOTES

PART THREE

Page 111. "...at the first congress of Muslim and Christian organizations..."

Yehoshua Porath, *The Palestinian Arab National Movement, 1929–1939: From Riots to Rebellion* (Vol. 2) (London: Frank Cass & Co. Ltd., 1977).

Page 113. "...this was preceded by appeals from Arab religious and political leaders..."

The New York Times, December 1, 1947.

J.C. Hurewitz, *The Struggle For Palestine* (New York: Schocken Books, 1976), 308.

Isi Leibler, *The Case For Israel* (Australia: The Executive Council of Australian Jewry, 1972), 15.

Page 114. "Just as no one should ignore the fate..."

Andrea Mifano, "The Expulsion of Jews from Arab Countries and Iran—An Untold Story," World Jewish Congress, February 2, 2021, https://www.worldjewishcongress.org/en/news/the-expulsion-of-jews-from-arab-countries-and-iran--an-untold-history.

Page 119. "...another group of new historians..."

David Motadel, *Islam and Nazi Germany's War* (Cambridge: Harvard University Press, 2014).

Matthias Küntzel, *Jihad and Jew-Hatred: Islamism, Nazism and the Roots of 9/11* (New York: Telos Press Publishing, 2007).

Jeffrey Herf, *Nazi Propaganda for the Arab World* (New Haven: Yale University Press, 2009).

Page 121. "'There are no Jews living in the Protectorate...'"

Tracy Wilkinson, "Is Zionism Patriotism or Racism? Big Disagreements Over a Word in Use for 125 Years," *The Los Angeles Times*, May 22, 2024, https://www.latimes.com/world-nation/story/2024-05-22/zionism-disagreement-over-a-word-in-use-for-125-years.

Page 122. "Then we have Amin al-Husseini…"

"The Grand Mufti of Jerusalem Advised Hitler Well on the Destruction of the Jews in Europe," *Slate*, October 25, 2015, https://www.slate.fr/story/108869/grand-mufti-jerusalem-hitler-destruction-juifs.

François-Guillaume Lorrain, "Hitler-Netanyahu-Mufti: The Historical Truth," *Le Point*, October 22, 2015, https://www.lepoint.fr/monde/hitler-netanyahu-mufti-la-verite-historique-22-10-2015-1975908_24.php.

Page 123. "…the fact that they had the 'same enemies'…"

"Full Official Record: What the Mufti Said to Hitler," *The Times of Israel*, October 21, 2015, https://www.timesofisrael.com/full-official-record-what-the-mufti-said-to-hitler/.

Page 128. "…which Israel was opening for several hours each day…"

Kevin Liptak, Alex Marquardt, and Jennifer Hansler, "Israel Will Begin 4-Hour Pause in Military Operations in Gaza Each Day, White House Says," CNN, November 9, 2023, https://www.cnn.com/2023/11/09/politics/israel-pauses-gaza-white-house/index.html.

Ilan Hulkower, "Israel Says It's Allowing Thousands of Gazans Through Humanitarian Corridor," *Daily Caller*, November 7, 2023, https://dailycaller.com/2023/11/07/israel-thousand-gazan-humanitarian-corridor-hamas-war/.

About the Author

BERNARD-HENRI LÉVY is a French philosopher, director of eight films, and author of forty-seven books. Lévy is one of the West's foremost intellectuals, defending democracy and humanism against totalitarianism and fascism. His recent books include *The Will to See: Dispatches from a World of Misery and Hope* (2021), *The Virus in the Age of Madness* (2020), *The Empire and the Five Kings* (2019), *The Genius of Judaism* (2017), *American Vertigo: Traveling America in the Footsteps of Tocqueville* (2005), and *Who Killed Daniel Pearl?* (2003).

Lévy has made films on the war in Bosnia; Libya; Iraqi Kurdistan besieged by ISIS; and Afghanistan, Somalia, Bangladesh, Nigeria, and Ukraine.

Lévy's work as an intellectual, a writer, and a filmmaker is intertwined with humanitarian activism. For fifty years, Lévy has reported on the world's "forgotten wars" and devoted numerous books, films, and articles to these crises. Lévy has participated in various Middle East peace initiatives and had contacts with Israeli leaders from Menachem Begin to Shimon Peres, and from Ariel Sharon to Yitzhak Shamir and Yitzhak Rabin.